Worldwide Acclaim for Leap Beyond Your Limits

"Anybody who wants to accomplish great things in his or her life should read this book! Chris explains the concepts of Inner-Forming" and Outer-Performing" so perfectly that they will have a profound effect on anyone who studies them."

—Paul Martinelli, featured in *Beyond the Secret*

"This book offers simple, easy-to-follow methods for achieving your goals from someone who actually lives what he teaches—Chris Curran."

—Roopa Rudrapatna, software engineer, and area governor, Toastmaster International

"Chris walks the walk, and he is somebody to follow. His extraordinary, but true, story is not only an inspiration but a roadmap to personal success for all of us."

—Shawn Collins, cofounder of Affiliate Summit Conference and copublisher of *FeedFront Magazine*

"*Leap Beyond Your Limits* is a thought-provoking, action-inducing read. You are compelled to look within yourself, take command, and rule your own future. Simply reading the words won't ensure your success; you must take ownership and action to live the life you dream. Curran outlines tools such as Inner-Forming˜ and Outer-Performing˜, tapping into your most powerful muscle—the mind—for a happy, productive, and healthy life."

—Kim S. Luthy, CLTC financial advisor,
Langdon Ford Financial

"Are you lost in a forest of past failures? Completely frustrated? No sense of direction? Relax, because Chris Curran's true rags-to-riches tale will lead you to all you want for your life. He maps out your route; helps you set a powerful, new direction; and shows you exactly how to create that 'success explosion' you crave. Chris has done everything but drop bread crumbs for you to follow. This book is clear, readable, informative, and entertaining ... and it is exactly what you need to succeed, case closed."

—Steven F. Miller, Business Strategies Group, LLC

"Chris's book sells for $29.95, but it's really priceless. After reading it, I realized I didn't just buy a book, I bought a road map to my future. I bought a lot of common sense and wisdom. I bought the best advice possible, and now I plan to put it into practice. As Chris writes, small changes produce major results in your business and personal life."

—Jeff Green, president, Pinnacle Graphic Communications

"This book will serve as a management tool for people of all ages and at all stages of their careers. It is a meaningful and useful guide to realizing your full potential and reaching beyond your self-imposed limitations."

—Kerrie R. Heslin, Esq., Nukk-Freeman & Cerra, P.C.

"Chris's book is an inspirational must-read, especially if you wish to take control of your life and achieve all your goals. Chris describes his unique and powerful two-part method for reaching your potential through Inner-Forming˜ and Outer-Performing˜, and he does so in a way that is easy to understand. Our subconscious minds are always at work, controlling our results every day; *Leap Beyond Your Limits* offers simple, yet practical lessons on how to develop new habits, how to shape your subconscious mind, and how to create the life you really want."

—Daryl H. Bryant, founder and president, Hudson Horizons
(http://www.HudsonHorizons.com)

"This book is powerful and inspiring. Chris Curran shows us exactly how the conscious and subconscious minds work together with his unique Inner-Forming˜ and Outer-Performing˜ theories. Reading this book was like watching the sun burn through a thick, dark fog until the world around me became crystal clear. I now know that I have absolute and total control over my own life. If you only read one book this year, you owe it to yourself to read *Leap Beyond Your Limits: How to Command and Rule Your Own Future*."

—Rocky Warren, author of *The Fighter Within*

"Too many people go through life as if it were a drill. They hold back, daydream, and wish for things others already have, but they're scared to try lest they fail. No one rides a bike with training wheels forever because we need challenge, excitement,… success! Chris reawakened my adventurous spirit, and his book will do the same for you. Come on. Remove those training wheels and *Leap Beyond Your Limits*."

—Bryant W. Jackson, musician and audio engineer
(http://www.BryantWJackson.com)

"Chris provides the tools you need to clearly understand universal laws and the action plan you need to accelerate your journey toward realizing your dreams. The concepts of Inner-Forming˘ and Outer-Performing˘ are life-changing. You will find yourself on a straight road to success, using your most powerful tool: your subconscious mind."

—Maria Mantoudakis, Dale Carnegie trainer, professional
speaker, and senior consultant at BT Americas

"Two of my favorite words in life are 'making connections.' Whenever I attend a seminar or read a book, I always look for those two or three gold nuggets, those wonderful 'pearls of wisdom' that I can take away and use throughout my life. *Leap Beyond Your Limits* is fascinating because it is a treasure chest filled to the brim with these gold nuggets. Chris explains perfectly his plan for Inner-Forming˘ and Outer-Performing˘. This book will help anyone grow as a person and be the best that they can possibly be. I believe this could be one of the best books you will ever read."

—Dan Hollis, director of sales, Grey Sky Films

"Chris reminds us that a positive visualization can drive a positive self-fulfilling prophecy and drive our lives. In order to keep control, we need to have a plan to implement our vision for positive results."

—Marty Finkle, CEO, Scotwork (NA) Inc., Negotiation Training and Consulting

"I've been helping leaders and teams achieve their goals for many years. *Leap Beyond Your Limits* delivers a powerful new angle of understanding that will help its readers realize their potential in their lives."

—Max Carbone, author of *Scoring Eagles*

"*Leap Beyond Your Limits* is a powerful book that forces us to take an honest look at our inner core. Chris Curran gives us the tools we need to truly reach our life potential. With his four mental arts, anyone can realize life success."

—Stefanie Conley, executive director, Dress for Success of Morris County, NJ

"Picture yourself lost in a strange, new city at night. No one speaks your language, and you never thought to bring a map. If that sounds like your life, you can now stop wandering around in endless circles. Chris Curran speaks your language in *Leap Beyond Your Limits,* and he's mapped out a plan to take you all the way to the good life you always wanted. This is a book that should be read often, not just once. Don't leave home without it."

—Christian Simpson, author of *Evolve ... Leadership Reinvented*

"Many of us go through life leaving success to chance, believing that a very successful person is 'lucky' and that someone achieving little success is 'unfortunate.' *Leap Beyond Your Limits* explains that success is very much something within your control. Chris explains how much influence your subconscious mind has over your life and how you can train it to help you succeed. If you want success, then I suggest you read this book."

—Brian Winkler, energy trader

"Chris Curran is a leader in the true sense of the word: he lives by his own example. Chris changed his mind and his mind-set and essentially recreated himself to become a successful entrepreneur. He's not a miracle worker; he's just a simple man with an extraordinary plan … and it works! Chris is the proof."

—Dr. James "Tad" Geiger, author of *The Sweet Smell of Success*

"Chris has a true gift and a passion for teaching people how to make the most of their lives. If you're looking for that elusive bridge between imagination and reality, this book will show you how to have it all. Its insights and timeless truths will put you on solid ground. Chris, you're a genius."

—Barry McGuire, technology professional, business consultant, and entrepreneur

LEAP
BEYOND YOUR
LIMITS

Glenn—
May you achieve all your
important goals, and always
keep your heart of gold!

LEAP

BEYOND YOUR
LIMITS

How to Command and Rule Your Own Future!

CHRIS CURRAN

LIFESUCCESS PUBLISHING, LLC
8900 E. Pinnacle Peak Road, Suite D240
Scottsdale, AZ 85255

Telephone:	800.473.7134
Fax:	480.661.1014
E-mail:	admin@lifesuccesspublishing.com
ISBN:	978-1-59930-342-0

Cover:	Eric Choi, LifeSuccess Publishing, LLC
Text:	Lloyd Arbour, LifeSuccess Publishing, LLC

Edit:	Publication Services Inc.

COMPANIES, ORGANIZATIONS, INSTITUTIONS, AND INDUSTRY PUBLICATIONS. Quantity discounts are available on bulk purchases of this book for reselling, educational purposes, subscription incentives, gifts, sponsorship, or fundraising. Special books or book excerpts can also be created to fit specific needs such as private labeling with your logo on the cover and a message from a VIP printed inside. For more information, please contact our Special Sales Department at LifeSuccess Publishing, LLC.

Inner-Forming™ and Outer-Performing™ are trademarked programs owned exclusively by Goal Ability, LLC

Printed in Canada

This book is dedicated to each and every member of the human race—past, present, and future.

Contents

Acknowledgments

Infinite love and gratitude to my spiritual guide, Parthasarathi Rajagopalachari.

For their essential and meaningful roles in my life,

I have great love and sincerest appreciation for:

My wife, Malar,

Mom and Dad,

my brothers, Mike, Matt, and Dan and my sister, Corinne,

all my aunts, uncles, cousins, nieces, nephews, and, of course, Grandma and Grandpa,

Bob Proctor, Paul Martinelli, and everyone at LifeSuccess Consulting, including all the other consultants and mentors, especially Christian Simpson, Roddy Galbraith, Brandon Dangerfield, and Paul Hutsey,

Gerry Robert, Wendy Gallagher, Wayne Collins, and everyone at LifeSuccess Publishing,

John Cogan, David Prudenti, Brian Winkler, Ian Grob, Bryant W. Jackson, Prakash Mahadevan, Shanmugam Chidambaranathan, and Dan Hollis.

Foreword

Often in my line of work, I am fortunate enough to become acquainted with individuals such as Chris Curran who, like myself, have found their true calling. Although I have only known Chris for a short while, his message, his passion, and his determination to help change lives are unquestionably radiating from the pages of *Leap Beyond Your Limits*.

Chris is most passionate about showing others how critically important it is to do the necessary inner work to achieve their external results. All the techniques and strategies in the world won't help if you don't have this inner strength of character as your foundation. His unique and powerful method—the balanced approach of Inner-Forming˝ and Outer-Performing˝—will allow anyone to stand tall, strong, and confident.

I wish I could say that most people truly understand the power the mind has to control and influence what happens in their lives, but, unfortunately, many do not. For many of us, changing a long-held opinion about someone else is quite difficult to manage. It can also be difficult for an individual to change the limiting opinions they hold about themselves. Chris's book is brilliant because it teaches you how to change that self-image, that mind-set, that roadblock you've built between you and your success.

Chris's own incredible rags-to-riches story should serve as a revelation to anyone who thinks success is only for other people and not themselves. Success is your birthright as much as anyone else's in this world. You really can change your life, as Chris shows, and you really can help other people change their lives too.

With extraordinary insight, Chris reveals clear-cut, step-by-step plans on how to develop consistency in your values, your beliefs, and your actions. You will learn the true value of integrity, how it enhances all your dealings with other people, and how it can open the door to the very life you've always imagined for yourself.

Far too many people focus on the negative aspects of their lives, forgetting they can just as easily pick and choose all the goodness that life has to offer. The time has come to change your opinion of yourself, to reach out and grab the opportunities around you. You now have the opportunity to begin accessing that wonderful, abundant, awesome power you are holding inside yourself. Read this book and really leap beyond your limits.

—**Bob Proctor,**
best-selling author of *You Were Born Rich*
and star of the hit movie, *The Secret*

Introduction

When he realizes that he is a creative power,
and that he may command
the hidden soil and seeds of his being
out of which circumstances grow,
he then becomes the rightful master of himself.

—James Allen

Everyone wants to be happier, earn more money, have more free time to spend with their family, friends, and hobbies, grow their business, travel more, etc., and I know *you* really want some of these things too. In order for you to achieve these things (soon enough to really enjoy them!), you're going to have to find ways to make small changes in your life that produce huge positive effects for you, and this is exactly what I present in this book: small changes that have big effects. If you understand and apply the simple concepts presented here, you will become a very powerful human being, and you will absolutely be able to achieve whatever you wish to achieve in your life.

I was a pretty happy kid growing up. I was an above-average student and very active in sports. After graduating high school, I went to one year of college and realized I didn't want to be in school any longer, so I went into the work force. I spent the next ten years working regular jobs. By the end of that ten-year period, I had gotten myself into quite a mess. I dug myself into a very deep financial and emotional hole. I ended up broke and unemployed, I had a mountain of debt, I had to give back my truck, and I couldn't even afford to renew the lease on my apartment. Have you ever felt frustrated, like you're spinning your wheels?

Luckily my friend offered his basement for me to live in, and I immediately took him up on his offer. During the time I lived in his basement, I lived through one of the coldest winters we've ever had, and let me tell you this basement had no heat. It was freezing! I had to wear at least five layers of clothing at all times, including five layers of socks. And in the middle of the night it was just arctic down there. I had to sleep with five big blankets *on top* of my five layers of clothing just to keep warm. Now imagine being in that situation in the middle of the night and then needing to go to the bathroom. It was brutal because by the time I hurried to the bathroom and came back, my bed was like a block of ice.

One of those nights after returning from the bathroom, as I lay there shivering trying to get warm—remember I was broke and unemployed—I silently, but earnestly, decided, *this is it. I can't live like this anymore. I'm going to change my life!* So the very next day, using the knowledge I had at the time, I designed my own success program.

I set my goals, created affirmations, and used other self-development techniques. I made a regimen for myself, and I followed it, and it really worked. Pretty soon I had a job and I was able to buy a cheap car. Within about six months, I was able to rent my own apartment again. Soon after that I got a much better job, and my income took off like a rocket. Around this time I got married too. I had literally turned my whole life around!

My success really excited me and got me thinking, "What am I *really* capable of?" I started studying and learning from hundreds of the smartest and wisest people in the world, and that studying led me to a man named Bob Proctor. Bob Proctor was featured in the films *The Secret* and *Beyond the Secret*. He's a renowned mentor of mentors—he has been in the personal development and human potential industry for almost 50 years!

I had the opportunity to meet with Bob, and eventually we became business partners. I followed my passion and gave up the security of a good job to start my company, Goal Ability (http://www.GoalAbility.com), and to devote the rest of my life to helping individuals and businesses create phenomenal results for themselves.

Using all my personal experience, along with the powerful material that Bob has gathered and assembled during his 50 years of success, I've created a unique and simple method you can use to unleash the best of your abilities and simply live the life you *really* want to live.

Within the pages of this book, after laying the necessary groundwork, I specifically describe my powerful two-part method: *Inner-Forming˝* and *Outer-Performing˝*. When you simultaneously apply both of these concepts to your own life, they behave like two elements in a chemical reaction—when you mix them together they cause an explosion! A success-explosion for you! Together they generate tremendous power. Inner-Forming˝ and Outer-Performing˝ are your twin engines of success, whether you're a business owner, a homemaker, an athlete, a salesperson, or anyone else.

I have worked passionately at creating this book, and I'm extremely happy to share the power in these pages with you. This book starts where it needs to start, with your current reality, and ends where it needs to end, showing you exactly what action steps to take so you can command and rule your own future.

Be brave; be open to new ideas. Allow the power inside yourself to be awakened. Your life is about to change—for the better.

There is only one success—to be able
to spend your life in your own way.

—Christopher Morley

1

Prelude to Progress

Healthy discontent is the prelude to progress.

—Mohandas Gandhi

In the film *The Replacements*, the character played by Keanu Reeves talks about his greatest fear. Previously he was a college quarterback who had lost a bowl game by a large margin and was accused of choking under the pressure. "Quicksand," he says. "You're playing and you think everything is going fine. Then one thing goes wrong. And then another. And another. You try to fight back, but the harder you fight, the deeper you sink. Until you can't move ... you can't breathe ... because you're in over your head. Like quicksand."

Is your life like that? Have you worked hard, believing that you're on the right track, and suddenly you look around and realize that you're trapped in quicksand? Not actual quicksand, but something just as dangerous—the quicksand of mediocrity.

Mediocrity as I use it here essentially means getting by or "surviving" instead of having what you really want or doing what you really want to do. You may be accepting mediocrity in your life in any number of ways:

- Not being able to purchase the things you'd like to purchase

- Not physically feeling as good as you'd like

- Not having as much free time as you'd like to spend with your family and on hobbies

- Not being able to travel as much as you'd like

- Not emotionally feeling as good as you'd like

What makes mediocrity so dangerous is that you may be mired in it without even realizing it. The same conditions that cause you to accept mediocrity can also blind you to it. The only way to know for sure is to take an honest look at yourself and where you are in your life.

Think first about the different roles you have to play: father, mother, brother, sister, son, daughter, member of a sales team, bowling league, or church. If you work with other people, you play a particular role in your office or business.

All of these roles come with differing expectations. In some of them you are expected to be a leader, in others a follower. To a child, you're expected to know everything; to a professor, you're expected to learn everything. You are likely expected to be warm and emotionally open in some roles, while in others emotionality is discouraged.

Think of how your different roles make you feel. Are you discouraged by your performance in some areas of your life? Do you feel unhappy with how a particular relationship is going? Do you wish you had closer bonds with some of the people you associate with?

Very few people have perfect lives, so don't expect to be 100 percent happy with each and every one of your roles. It helps to look at your life from two different perspectives. When you look at the **small picture**, what do you see? How do you spend your days? Performing activities that excite and energize you? Or trudging through each day with one eye on the clock, waiting for the first chance to go home?

When you take a look at your life from the **big picture,** how does your life look compared to five years ago? Ten years ago? Twenty? Do you see more or less steady improvement from one decade to the next? Or do you see stagnation or even a decline in your quality of life?

It helps to have measuring sticks to gauge where you are at in life. Income is certainly one valid way to measure your quality of life. Looking at your income gives you the advantage of using concrete numbers as a measurement. It's hard to dispute that $50,000 is less than $100,000. Although some years may be better than others, over a long period of time you should see a steady increase.

Another measurement is your physical health. Do you suffer from lifestyle-related conditions, such as obesity, high blood pressure, or alcoholism? Do you feel energized when you wake up in the mornings, or do you have to drag yourself out of bed and through your day? Do you get plenty of exercise, feel mentally alert, and participate in outside activities?

It's always helpful to take an inventory of your skills, talents, ambitions, and plans. Playing to your strengths is one of the surest routes not only to success but to personal fulfillment on all levels. For example, Michael Jordan was one of the greatest basketball players in the history of the National Basketball Association. As a Minor League Baseball player, however, he was not quite as successful. His work ethic, physical attributes, and desire to win were not enough to make him a great baseball player—his strengths lay on the basketball court.

In the same way, you may be using your strengths in the wrong field, or not even using your strengths at all. By taking an inventory of your individual strengths and talents, you can make an honest decision of whether you are doing the best job with the tools you have at your disposal.

The key to any self-assessment, of course, is honesty. You will often find that the same characteristics that leave you mired in mediocrity can make it impossible for you to look at yourself honestly. That's why objective measurements such as your pay and your health are easier to measure than subjective matters, e.g., how happy you are.

Happiness

Happiness can be difficult to define. Sure, you know your happy when you're feeling good, but even *feeling good* can mean different things. You may feel good right after you've eaten a big meal, full of carbohydrates and fat, but then feel miserable when you realize that you are overweight and have been trying to diet. Another error you could make is by mistaking *satisfied* for *happy*. Satisfaction often means simply an absence of pain. Absence of pain is good, of course, but living a full life should mean more than not hurting.

One definition of happiness is when you are living your life in accordance with your values. Values are principles or concepts that are most important to you. They form the basis of what kind of person you are. Valuing concepts such as honesty, courage, faith, hope, and charity will lead you to a higher plane of living.

If one of your core values is that it is virtuous to work hard, but you take it as easy as possible, then you will likely not feel completely happy. When you act and live in conflict with your values and beliefs, then you're living a lie. You may be the only one who knows it, but when it comes to deciding if you are happy or not, you're the only one that matters.

Take a look at your personal life. Are you honest, open, and forthright with those close to you? Or do you feel compelled to keep secrets from everyone? Do you look forward to spending time with your family and friends, or do you approach each get-together with dread? After such occasions, do you leave revitalized, or are you drained, exhausted, and relieved that it's over?

In your professional life, deciding if you're happy is simpler in some ways, and more complex in others. You know if you've been passed over for promotions, missed out on bonuses, or received raises that were smaller than you expected (or even no raises at all!). More subtle than money and rank is how you actually feel about what you do. Are you proud to tell people what kind of work you do? Or do you feel compelled to make excuses for your job?

A fundamental key to change is having the willingness to ask yourself basic questions. When you ask yourself these questions, you are already ahead of most people. Our society today is so busy that we don't spend much time on quiet introspection. We dash from one appointment to the next without ever asking if they are the best way to spend our time.

Stopping to answer the question *Am I happy?* doesn't sound like a radical idea, but it's a question that few people give any real thought to. As Henry David Thoreau said more than 150 years ago, "The mass of men lead lives of quiet desperation." If that description feels familiar to you, then it's time you asked yourself some questions.

If you're like most people, you are probably happy with some things in your life and not so happy with others. The next question you have to ask yourself is *Am I where I want to be?* Is your situation in life where you imagined it would be when you were a child? Children are visionaries—they haven't dealt with the disappointments and frustrations of life yet, so their hopes and dreams are still pure. They admire bravery, so they want to be astronauts or police officers. They crave adventure, so they want to be cowboys or explorers.

You're not a child any more, of course, but you can still live up to your dreams. Are you living up to your potential, or do you feel in your heart that there's more you can do in life? Each of us has strengths—are you using yours? Are you living an extraordinary life, or do you feel as though greatness is beyond you? You might be surprised at what you're capable of.

Ismael "Mel" Feneque found out what he was capable of when he saw Lisa Donath fall onto the subway tracks in Manhattan. Still groggy from donating blood the night before, Lisa collapsed and fell from the platform onto the tracks only moments before a train was scheduled to thunder through. Feneque jumped into the path of the coming train and lifted her back up onto the platform. He barely escaped death, lifting himself out of the way with inches to spare.

Why did Mel Feneque, an ordinary man, commit such an act of bravery to help a stranger? "All I know" he said, "is I was there, and I'd do it again."

Not Where You Want to Be

One of the common definitions of insanity is to do the same thing over and over and expect a different result. Your situation (your place) is a result of the series of decisions you have made in your life. If you are not where you want to be in life, then the things you have done and the actions you have taken to get to this place aren't working for you. To repeat the same pattern and expect your life to improve would be, by the above definition, insanity.

There could be several reasons for you to be someplace you don't want to be. Maybe you had a good plan, but you executed it poorly. You might have had a poor plan and executed it perfectly. If you're like most people, though, you didn't have a plan at all. Most people don't take the time to think and plan before they decide what to do with their lives. Sometimes people fail to plan because they simply don't know what they want. If you don't know what you want, there's nothing to plan *for*.

You may have had legitimate obstacles along the way that kept you from achieving your goals in the exact way you thought you would. Physical and mental disabilities make some courses of action more difficult. If you want to use obstacles as an excuse for not achieving your goals, then maybe you should watch the Paralympics sometime. World-class athletes compete in different events, just as in the regular Olympics. In the Paralympics, however, the athletes are amputees or sufferers of disabilities such as cerebral palsy or spinal cord injuries. Many of the athletes compete in wheelchairs. They achieve top physical performance despite their disabilities through sheer hard work and perseverance.

Do the obstacles that you have had to face compare to those of these athletes?

Most people don't face those kinds of obstacles in their lives. More often, they run into a slight obstacle and give up. A mind-set that tells you *I can't do it* or *this is too hard* can keep you knee-deep in mediocrity for the rest of your life. Successful people become successful because they are willing to do what the average person won't do. *Giving up* is not in their vocabulary.

If you're not where you want to be, and you have an idea of why not, then why would you keep doing what you're doing? Some people stick to their guns out of stubbornness, unwilling to face facts, especially the fact that they haven't accomplished all they could.

A few people—very few—repeat their self-defeating patterns over and over out of ignorance. Not only are they not self-aware but they are also oblivious to the world around them. They will often make minor changes in their actions, thinking that they are adjusting to the world, but they can't tell that they are simply doing the same things over.

The most common reason that we don't change what we're doing is also the most tragic. It's when we simply give up and accept what life has dealt us, regardless of how painful or empty our lives are. Apathy and resignation destroy more lives than any disease.

What Holds You Back

The question you may be asking yourself now is *Why do I stay mediocre? Why don't I break out of this habit of "less than success?"* First of all, you have to understand that, by definition, you are surrounded by average people. Everyone wants to fit in, to conform, and the easiest way to accomplish that is to be "average."

We are often held back by the desires of those closest to us. Family and friends have their own image of you, a pigeonhole where they have put you. If you try to improve your life, you may shake their world by changing that image, the one that they have become comfortable with. They may feel that they are "losing" you and, in their affection, try to keep you close. They can only do that by trying to force you back into the pigeonhole from which you're trying to escape.

Perhaps you may have learned to accept the pain of mediocrity. Change only happens when your dissatisfaction with your life situation becomes unbearable, forcing you to decide on a new course of action. Remember me in that arctic basement? Unfortunately, most of us have a high tolerance for the sort of emotional and spiritual pain that comes with living a lesser life. We may rationalize our inaction—we're too old, too young, too fat, too thin, too something—simply to hide the pain from ourselves. Ultimately though, the pain of underachieving becomes a dull ache that stays with you day and night.

There are two main problems with accepting mediocrity. First, the clock is ticking. You have a finite amount of time on earth. Some people have more time, some have less, but each of us is allotted only a certain amount of time. You have a limited amount of time to accomplish everything that you dreamed of as a child and to achieve everything that you are capable of now. By accepting mediocrity you are squandering that time, and every minute that you waste is gone forever, never to be regained.

The second problem with mediocrity is that it's infectious. Once you have accepted it in one part of your life, it tends to permeate every other aspect of your life. Although no one can be exceptional in everything they do, doing the best job you can in all your roles is something anyone can strive for. By accepting less than your best in one area, you will find it easier to start doing less than your best in all areas. Mediocrity becomes a habit.

Eventually mediocrity will destroy your life. You will constantly be passed over for promotions, bonuses, and other perks of your job. You may find yourself in an unrewarding, unfulfilling relationship. Other people will ignore your ideas when you speak up in a meeting.

The worst part of underachieving and acceptance of our low performance is that we know that it's self-inflicted. By our actions, we are choosing to live a life of disappointment, frustration, and pain. In the back of your mind, you may realize that you feel empty and unfulfilled, as though something is missing in your life.

Don't fool yourself into believing that those around you can't see your disappointment. Only those in complete denial can think that the people around them can't see their life. You give clues to others that communicate how you feel about your life. Body language, sounds you make, and offhand comments made without thinking tell the people around you how you feel—if you are proud of what you are and what you do, or if you feel trapped.

Although one television commercial says that others judge you by the words you use (and they do), they base their judgments more on how you feel about yourself and how you act. As John Locke said, "I have always thought the actions of men the best interpreters of their thoughts." Whether they want to or not, the people around you form an impression of you—judge you—and find a place in their mental world where you will fit.

In your business life, your coworkers decide if you are a benefit to the team or if you drag it down. Even if your results are not directly dependent on the efforts of others, the people you report to and the others with whom you interact will seek you out if that interaction is beneficial to them and will avoid you if being around you is negative.

Within You

Mediocrity is the incorrect application of inaccurate knowledge. Within you lies the possibility of greatness, the ability to make much more of your life than you have so far. Deep down you know this is true. Your ideas of yourself may be holding you back, or you may simply lack the techniques that will make the best use of the skills, talents, and abilities that you have inside you. You have limited yourself because of what you've been told by others or by incorrectly interpreting events that have happened to you.

Before we lay out the ideas and principles that will give you whatever you want in life (and how to implement them), we first must have a good understanding of ourselves and what's really going on inside of us. Over the next two chapters we'll lay the groundwork for tapping into your deep power.

Success is the manifestation of your actions, and your actions are the manifestation of your thoughts. Success, then, springs from the thoughts and mental processes that you exert. For you to become the true commander and ruler of your own future, you must first understand the very process that creates *all* the results in your future.

2

The Birthplace of All Your Actions

*Nature has endowed man with absolute control
over but one thing, and that is THOUGHT.*

—Napoleon Hill

When we are stuck in one place due to indecision, we often hear the advice "Don't think, do!" That advice is certainly sound in many instances. Success requires action. To continue our quicksand analogy, you have to do something to pull yourself out of the muck of mediocrity. However, for an action to be successful (other than accidentally,) somebody *somewhere* has to do some thinking.

The panicky flailing of your arms and legs in quicksand will merely drag you lower. If you relax, however, you will find that your body will tend to float, just as in water. In this case, a moment of calmness and thought beats pointless activity. If someone else is nearby, they may throw you a rope, and you can escape that way.

Success is the result of action, but not all action results in success. The mental process is important because you want to direct your energy toward actions that increase your likelihood of success. Not only does using your mind increase your likelihood of success but when you put some thought into your actions *before* you actually execute them, you will find that your life is much simpler.

Once when I was a boy, I wanted to rearrange the furniture in my bedroom. I wasn't really sure how I wanted it to be, so before expending a lot of energy actually moving the heavy furniture around several times to figure out the setup I wanted, I carefully measured all the furniture in my room, as well as the room itself. I then made a scale model of everything by cutting up bits of paper. I used the scale model to play around with possible configurations until I discovered the arrangement I liked. It worked like a charm, and then I moved the furniture. Once.

You are probably a hard worker; you energetically attack tasks, make to-do lists, and zoom through your day. Time for a reality check—how's all that activity working for you?

This brings to mind the proverb of the French Foreign Legion: *When in doubt, gallop!*

The truth is, most plans don't work. Even in the highly-formalized world of professional football where computers calculate tendencies of the other teams and coaches have thick books of plays for their offense to run, only a few of the plays result in touchdowns. Most plays gain only a few yards and occasionally result in lost yardage.

With all the technological and scientific data professional teams have at their disposal, they still can't design perfect game plans. How are you, with your few resources, supposed to reach your goals? Why don't the plans you create work for you like they're supposed to?

For one thing, you may be using the wrong plan. If you are a salesperson and you want to increase your sales, you may decide to increase the number of clients you call on each day. If your problem is that you don't call on enough people, then the extra effort may pay off. But what if the problem is not the number of people you contact, but poor sales technique? Your time will be spent wasting potential customers.

Another example is that if you want a better relationship with your children, you may determine that you are going to spend an extra half hour a day with them. That's an admirable goal, and parents should spend as much time with their kids as they can. If you have a troubled teenager—almost a given these days—then he or she may be trying to exert his or her independence and might feel as though you are checking up on him or her by taking away precious free time. Your well-intentioned efforts may result in the complete opposite effect of what you intended.

Managers and supervisors know that proper training of their staff is a key component of a successful company. If you are in a supervisory capacity, you may decide that you will spend an extra hour a week on training. The staff, on the other hand, may have their own ideas of how their time should be spent and view that hour not as self-development but as more time wasted in meetings. Your training efforts fall on deaf ears and unreceptive minds, resulting in a team that not only is untrained but actually resists and resents training.

All of these are examples of wrong plans, wrong methods, and poor execution. With a little thought and a few questions, all of them—with some adjustments—could lead to success. The sales professional might look at his or her sales technique or closing ratio. The concerned parent can ask questions, or even better, simply listen. The manager can ask the staff where they feel they need the most training and design the program around their answers.

The problem, then, is not with planning, but with bad planning. The same principle applies to your efforts to your own personal success. A good plan works better than a bad plan, but no plan is the worst of all. As the old saying goes, failing to plan is planning to fail.

What causes you to make bad plans? Limited thinking.

Limited Thinking

Limited thinking is exactly what it sounds like—thoughts that limit your success, that prevent you from reaching the greatest heights to which you are capable. Limited thinking takes varied forms, but those variations are almost always a manifestation of one thing: restricted vision. Placing limits on yourself blinds you to all the options that are open to you. It's as though you only see single colors and not the entire rainbow of potential that awaits you.

This obliviousness, or lack of awareness, is not due to any sort of mental impairment. It's a spiritual blindness that can afflict anyone. Most people suffer from it to one degree or another in some part of their life. A few people are lucky enough to wear blinders in just a few of their roles, and the truly fortunate ones are those who recognize that they have blinders on and work to overcome that handicap.

Sometimes the lack of awareness of options is not due to lack of attention, but occurs when we have convinced ourselves that there is only one way to do something. Our focus on that one option is so strong that we don't realize that there may be other, better ways to accomplish our ultimate goal.

During World War II, fighter pilots often suffered from a syndrome known as *target fixation*. As they used their machine guns on targets on the ground, they became so focused on a particular target that they forgot to pull up, often crashing into the ground. Many pilots made it back to their airfield with mud on the bottom of their planes.

Take a moment to think back on some times when you were unable to reach your goal, or you reached it only after what seemed an inordinate amount of effort. Was your lack of effectiveness due to target fixation? Did you take the longer or more difficult route to achieve your goal, when another method—just as effective, but easier—was open to you? If so, then you expended unnecessary energy, energy that could have been devoted to reaching another goal.

Limited thinking can be caused by many things, but essentially it boils down to *false beliefs*. False beliefs are patterns that have been imprinted on you at some point in your life and that negatively influence how much of your mind is available to help you reach your goals. These patterns are imprinted onto your subconscious mind in childhood in emotional or stressful situations or when a trusted authority plants them.

There's a story of a young musician who once approached a famous violinist. The young man begged the violinist to listen to him play. "I want to pursue music as a career," the young man said. "If you can confirm for me that I have the talent, I will devote myself to my playing." The violinist motioned for him to play.

The young musician had only played for a moment when the violinist stopped him. "Give it up. You lack the fire." The young man was crushed, but he accepted the maestro's verdict. He put away his violin and studied business, eventually becoming a very successful businessman.

Years later, he ran into the old violinist again. "I want to thank you," he said. "If not for your words, I would have wasted my life playing music, instead of choosing a career in business. I've wondered, though, how you could tell I lacked the fire from listening to me play for just a few moments?"

The old man nodded. "I remember you. I barely listened to you play. Whenever young musicians want to play for me, I always tell them that they lack the fire."

"What? That's awful! You changed my life completely. I could have been a world-class violinist like yourself! I could have played in front of huge crowds in the greatest auditoriums in the world."

The old man shook his head. "You misunderstand. If you had the fire, you would have paid no attention to me. If you had the fire, nothing anyone said could have stopped you from achieving your dream."

Sometimes our beliefs are based on the wrong sources. Through laziness or apathy, we follow a shallow philosophy, often based on a proverb. The problem with most proverbs is that they are only applicable in certain situations. For example, you may have heard the proverb that you can't teach an old dog new tricks. If you buy into this philosophy, then at whatever age you consider old (and that point changes the older you get!) you subconsciously give yourself permission to stop learning. When you stop learning, you stop growing.

The universe constantly changes around us, and what once worked may no longer work. New conditions call for new solutions, or old solutions adapted to the new conditions. The benefit of experience is that it gives you a larger database of possible solutions to choose from. But you have to be flexible enough in your thinking to realize that you may have to learn something new in order to implement an appropriate solution. Basing your beliefs on a proverb alone limits your possibilities.

Working with a set of true, useful beliefs is vital to arriving at important decisions and proper courses of action. (*Useful*, in the context of this book, refers to those actions, thoughts, or attitudes that move you toward accomplishing your goals.) As we've seen, false or negative beliefs can cripple your efforts at achieving success.

Despite our chaotic lives and the jumbled picture we sometimes have of our minds, it's not difficult to create an understanding that can move you closer to success. We simply take the complex process of making plans and break it down to its basic components. The structure of thought that you need to form successful plans is based on three levels of mind function: your *beliefs*, your *thoughts*, and your *conclusions*.

Beliefs

Beliefs are those things in your life that you accept as true without evidence. The earth is round—unless you're an astronaut who has been in orbit, you don't have direct evidence to corroborate that fact. You simply accept it as true, and that acceptance has worked fine for you whenever you needed it. Your belief in the earth's shape has been useful to you, whether on a test when you were in grade school or when calculating intercontinental trajectories or flight plans.

On the other hand, some beliefs are less useful. If you were a teenager whose parents and grandparents never went to college, whose aunts and uncles never went to college, and who lived in a neighborhood where no one had ever gone to college, then you might believe that "people like you" don't go to college. You accept this point as a fact, a fundamental belief. By accepting this belief, you structure your actions and attitude around not going to college. This belief has been less useful because it has limited your options.

Beliefs are the foundational concepts upon which all else rests. Based on your beliefs, you engage in certain thoughts and not others. You arrive at some conclusions without reaching others. Your beliefs are the roots of your behavior. All of your actions are simply the physical manifestations of the process that begins with your beliefs.

A simple example of a belief is in a deductive statement (called a *syllogism*) such as you would see in the world of logic: All men are mortal. Socrates is a man. Therefore Socrates is mortal. When you accept the initial statement, *all men are mortal*, then you have established a premise or belief. Without that belief, you could not have arrived at the conclusion that Socrates is mortal.

Beliefs can work for you or against you. Negative beliefs are often phrased as "all or nothing" statements: "I always mess up when I'm under pressure" or "I never finish anything I start." Either of these statements may fall apart under closer inspection, but it takes conscious effort to look at your beliefs to determine their validity and usefulness.

Beliefs are based on our values, and those values can fall anywhere on a spectrum. Very few of us hold an extreme belief when it comes to ethical, moral, or philosophical statements. Most of us fall somewhere in the middle area of most debates. At times, it's even possible to have your values conflict. Consider these two statements:

"The first requisite of a good citizen in this republic of ours is that he shall be able and willing to pull his own weight," from Theodore Roosevelt.

"Down in their hearts, wise men know this truth: the only way to help yourself is to help others." from Elbert Hubbard.

These two statements are both expressions of values and would seem to contradict one another, yet they don't. Most people would probably combine the two to form a thought along the line of, "Take care of yourself as much as possible, and help as many other people as you can." As values go, that's not a bad statement. It combines two concepts that most people respect: hard work and generosity.

It can be useful to look at your innermost values and evaluate them. Find out if the values you hold are ones you're proud of. If one of your beliefs is "Hard work is for suckers," then you have automatically limited your options to those that don't involve hard work. The process of examining your values and beliefs can be enlightening, so take the time to look inside yourself to see what you're basing your thoughts on.

Thoughts

If beliefs are the roots of the process you use to make decisions, then your *thoughts* are the leaves. Thoughts are conscious glimpses of perception that determine your course of action. Based on your beliefs, you have certain thoughts and not others, and you are unaware of the thoughts you don't have. (Because if you were *aware* of them, then they would be thoughts that you *have*.)

Ideas come to us as a result of our beliefs interacting with our environment. If we perceive something that conflicts with one of our beliefs, we discard it. If you believe in ghosts and a chair moves across the room, then you may have the idea that a ghost just moved the chair. If you don't believe in ghosts, then you look for other explanations for the phenomenon—an earthquake, a tilted floor, a gust of wind, or something else. The idea that a ghost moved furniture doesn't even enter your mind.

On a more practical level, what if you hold the belief—programmed into you as a child—that you are fat? If you are lonely, you may attribute your loneliness to your self-image as a fat person. The reality may be that you have an abrasive personality that repels people, or you may be extremely shy and don't put yourself in social situations where you can meet people. If you have decided, based on your beliefs, that you're lonely because you are fat, then you don't look for other explanations that might be more accurate.

Although our thoughts are based on our beliefs, they must also have an environment that provides information. In our modern world, we are buried in information. Television, movies, magazines, newspapers, and the Internet all combine to create a huge universe of impressions that impose on us. In the previous example, for instance, the person decided that the cause of his or her loneliness was weight. This decision is reinforced by the images of svelte movie stars and models, by articles in nearly every magazine on how to lose weight, and possibly comments that other people have made.

With the glut of information that we suffer from in modern society, more of our thoughts are formed based on the experience of others rather than on our own personal experiences. The amount of exposure that most people have to different forms of media has a cumulative impact on the way they see the world.

The influence the media has on us results in our thinking a lot of "I ought to" thoughts. Based simply on what they see in the movies or on television, viewers decide that their own lives lack something and that they ought to do something about it. Advertisers take advantage of this vulnerability to the human psyche. Their messages are full of false thoughts.

If we watch commercials on television, we think we ought to speak to our doctor about a new medicine, we ought to drive a new car, and we ought to go eat a hamburger when we go to lunch. Like negative or false beliefs, these false thoughts are designed only to manipulate your behavior. The sheer quantity of these manipulative messages makes it impossible to properly evaluate each and every one of them.

For that reason alone, it's important that you take time to "unplug" occasionally. Provide some quiet time for yourself so that you can sort out your own thoughts and ideas without the clamor of advertising, movies, or other media. If you are looking for higher-quality thoughts, then you need to provide a proper environment to develop them. Tony Robbins puts it simply: "If you want to improve the quality of your life, improve the quality of your questions."

Thoughts are habitual. If you are in the habit of feeding your brain hours and hours of television, then your thoughts will reflect this. On the other hand, if you are in the habit of regularly engaging in contemplative, deep self-examination, then your thoughts will also reflect it.

You can also improve the quality of your thoughts by getting in the habit of reading uplifting or motivational books, listening to uplifting music, or engaging in conversation with people whose outlooks are uplifting or inspiring. You may have heard the old saying about computers, "Garbage in, garbage out." The opposite is also true. If you put quality into your mind, then you'll get quality results out.

Conclusions

Conclusions are the course of action or inaction that we choose to pursue based on our beliefs and thoughts. They are the decisions we make. If beliefs are the roots and thoughts are the leaves, then conclusions are the fruit of the mental process. In terms of logic, we can use the expression "because of a and b, then c." In other words, because of our beliefs and our thoughts, then we arrive at this conclusion.

Using our previous example, your belief might be that you're fat. Your thought would be that you're lonely because you're fat. Based on these two factors, you arrive at the conclusion that you won't try to establish new relationships. Your limited thoughts have led you to accepting defeat before you even try.

Generally, limiting conclusions are phrased in terms of *can't*: "I *can't* meet new people" or "I *can't* increase my sales." The mind-set of these conclusions is one of defeat, helplessness, and fatalism. People who accept conclusions such as this basically relieve themselves of any responsibility for their situation. Since they *can't* do something, then it's not their fault if things don't go their way. This type of rationalization eases the pain of mediocrity.

As Henry Ford once said, "Whether you think you can or think you can't, you're right."

Changing the Equation

The three components of planning—beliefs, thoughts and conclusions—are the components of an equation. Beliefs lead to thoughts, which lead to conclusions. If you take any of those components out of the equation, the others exist in a vacuum. This equation, or process, generates the plans we make for our life and ultimately determine our results.

If you want to change your life, you have to change the equation. That means changing the factors that result in your decisions, and that means changing your beliefs. Our beliefs are buried deep in our subconscious mind. You may hold beliefs that you never knew you had. The goal is to discover your beliefs and adjust them. As a wise man once said, "You have to water the roots of the plant, not the leaves." You can't form good thoughts on bad beliefs.

As you establish useful beliefs, you will find that your thoughts begin to change also. Pay attention to the feedback you receive on your thoughts—do they make you feel better? Do they seem to open up possibilities, rather than limit your choices?

When you adjust your beliefs and your thoughts, then better conclusions will naturally follow. The quality of your decisions will improve, and you will find that you have more resources at your disposal. Instead of thinking *can't,* you will focus on how to make something happen. Even more important is that you will have a stronger *why.* Instead of trying to live your life down with negative beliefs and thoughts, you will be aspiring to a higher level of existence.

Before we can get into the exact details of how to change your mental-process equation (and therefore your results), it's crucial to go one level deeper to understand the very source of your individual power. You'll gain a critical understanding of that amazing mind you have, and then you'll learn exactly how you can effectively command it.

3
The Power of the Mind

Progress is impossible without change,
and those who cannot change their minds
cannot change anything.

—George Bernard Shaw

Everything begins with the mind. In his book *The 8th Habit: From Effectiveness to Greatness*, Stephen Covey says, "All things are created twice: first a mental creation; second a physical creation." Nothing we do happens in the real world without first being conceived in the mind. Consider all the masterworks of art and literature, all the wonderful inventions, all the acts of bravery, generosity, and kindness—the scope of what the human mind is capable of is staggering.

As we consider the power of the mind, it's important to separate the concept of the mind from the image of the brain. Although the brain is the physical organ in which our thoughts occur, it is only the physical image. The mind is not actually an *it*; it's not something that you can see or hold in your hands. The mind is more of a process. The brain has the tissue, the capillaries, the nerve endings, and all the other physical features that doctors study in medical school. The mind manifests itself in other ways—in the works of art, inventions, and acts of virtue I mentioned above.

It's easy to get distracted and confused by the difference. Most of us have seen the end of the movie *The Wizard of Oz*, where the scarecrow approaches the wizard and asks for a brain. The great Wizard presents the scarecrow with a diploma, whereupon the scarecrow spouts a mathematical equation. The scarecrow never actually *got* a brain, he simply started thinking. For movie audiences, though, the diploma visually represented the brain, or to be more precise, the *workings* of the brain—the mind.

The brain can be studied. Scientists measure its electrical output as it works, surgeons use scalpels or lasers to tinker with various parts of it, and safety experts suggests we wear helmets so we don't injure it. However, with all of those educated people working with, on, and around the brain, none of them can tell you where the mind is. If they're being honest, they will admit that they don't understand the workings of the mind at all. They only know the physical brain.

The question that often comes up is, "Do we use all of our brain's power?" A common belief is that human beings use only about 10 percent of their brain. I'm sorry to burst that bubble, but scientists using advanced electronic equipment have conducted studies that have shown that healthy people use all of their brain at one point or another.

What scientists have not measured is how much of the *mind* humans use. How do you measure the flashes of intuition, perception, or inspiration that happen to us? Scientists can only theorize about what causes the savants (such as the one portrayed by Dustin Hoffman in the movie *Rain Man*) to have the phenomenal ability to calculate huge numbers, exhibit complete recall of a scene, or reproduce a complex melody after hearing it only once.

During brain surgery, the patient is often kept awake while the surgeon operates. During this "wide awake" brain surgery, a surgeon can stimulate a part of the brain, and the patient will suddenly recall a scene or event from the distant past in great detail. What this means is that it is possible for us to have total recall—that every event is recorded somewhere in our mind—if we only have the means to retrieve it.

To be sure, some people have developed their memories to a tremendous degree. If you are familiar with the game of chess, then you know it is tremendously complicated. Thirty-two pieces on sixty-four squares create a lot of possibilities, even just for the first few moves. The mathematical possibilities for the number of moves in an entire game are astronomical. Blindfold chess is a form of chess where the players conduct the entire game in their minds, without sight of the board or pieces. Sounds tough, huh?

The world record for blindfold chess is held by Janos Flesch, who conducted 52 games simultaneously. In a 12-hour display, Flesch won 31 games, drew 3, and lost 18. Compared to the difficulty we sometimes have remembering everything we need to get at the supermarket, Flesch's feat is mind-boggling. He developed his memory to a point that most of us have never even dreamed of.

In addition to feats of prodigious memorization, the human mind is capable of many other phenomena described under the collective term *genius*. Experts have established that there are many different types of genius in addition to the common idea of someone who scores high on IQ tests. What the act of genius ultimately means, though, is the ability to see the world differently, combining elements in a way that has never been seen before.

Geniuses and savants are tapping into the power of their mind a bit more effectively or efficiently than the rest of us and accomplishing amazing feats or creating brilliant works of art. If we can learn to use our minds more effectively, could we be capable of great achievements, as well? That touch of genius occurs the first time you can genuinely look ahead and see yourself living a better life, more successful in every way. Creating that viewpoint is the first step toward mastery of your mind.

One other point about the human mind: the human being is the only creature on earth that is self-aware and understands that it has the capacity to change. Animals have brains, and many of them are highly intelligent. However, animals act on instinct (except when they've been taught a new behavior by a human). Man is the only creature that can consciously change its circumstances.

Two Parts of the Mind

When we talk about *consciousness*, what do we mean? The word *conscious* comes from the Latin *conscious*, meaning "to know." To be conscious of something means that you are aware of it. Therefore, conscious thoughts are those that you are aware of. There are an infinite number of thoughts you can have, from thinking about your next sales call to trying to remember the name of someone you met, to calculating your income tax. What they all have in common is that you are aware of what you are thinking.

The conscious mind is where your thoughts are structured. We can try to control, direct, or manage our thoughts, but as we saw in the previous chapter, the thoughts that are available to us at any given time are provided by our beliefs and habits, which reside in the subconscious mind. In this sense, the conscious mind is the little brother of the subconscious mind.

The subconscious is the silent partner of the mind. The conscious mind is the great storyteller that impresses people at parties with jokes and anecdotes, while the subconscious is laboring away, making sure that everything underneath is performing efficiently. If there is one lesson to take away from this section, it's that *the subconscious mind is always working.*

First off, the subconscious mind takes care of all the autonomic functions of your body. If you had to think about making your heart beat or think about breathing, you wouldn't have any attention left to commit to the rest of your environment. The subconscious mind makes it possible for you to physically exist in the world. In more ways than one, it is the major component of the mind-body connection.

As we have learned previously, the subconscious mind is the seat of all your belief systems and habits. Through patterns that were established in you at some previous time, you hold certain things to be true, and you have organized your physical world around these beliefs. The way you organize your world is what forms your habits. If your belief is that breakfast is the most important meal of the day, then you have likely formed the habit of eating breakfast every morning, and probably at about the same time every day. If that is not one of your beliefs, then you may grab something on the way to work if you have the chance or even skip breakfast all together. Your habits are formed by your beliefs.

In this sense, then, your subconscious mind controls your results. In its most basic form, success is the result of performing successful actions. If you perform successful actions consistently—if you've developed the *habit* of doing them—then your likelihood of success is very high.

Since the subconscious mind is always working—like the old Pinkerton Detective Agency, whose motto was "We never sleep"—

every experience you've ever had made an impression on your subconscious. To one degree or another, each experience has had an emotional effect on you. It brought you either pain or pleasure. The associations you have now are based on the emotional impacts made at earlier times.

One example is if you were attacked by a dog when you were a small child. It might have even been a small dog, but an experience like that can lead to your being afraid of dogs as an adult. The pain of the earlier experience carries over into the present, bypassing the conscious mind and its language ("I'm bigger than that dog. He's not going to bite me. He's on a leash"), and directly affects your central nervous system.

Overcoming a fear like this is possible, and many people do it. Traditionally it takes an enormous amount of effort and work to reorganize your subconscious feelings so that something that scared you years ago no longer has the same effect now. However, by using the *Inner-Forming* techniques in this book, it is much easier, although it still takes work.

Recognizing Patterns

We have different types of memory. Researchers Chase and Simon conducted a study with a group of chess players in the 1970s. The participants were divided into two groups: masters and beginners. The participants were briefly shown a position from an actual chess game, then asked to recreate the position. The masters consistently scored much higher than the beginners.

However, when the pieces were placed randomly on the board in positions that would never come up in a real game, there was no difference in the accuracy of the two groups. In the first instance, the masters had been able to recognize patterns based on their ability and their experience.

The subconscious mind works in the same way—it establishes patterns to create responses in our body. Have you ever glanced at a shadow and jumped, thinking that it was a spider? After your conscious mind turns its attention to the matter, you can see that it's just a shadow. But your first reaction was based on your subconscious mind's ability to create a pattern (dark, shadowy, creepy, looks like it has a lot of legs) and a response before your conscious mind had time to kick in.

This is an important concept. Your subconscious mind communicates through images, emotions, and associations. If a new situation arises, the subconscious mind provides a similar pattern—accurate or not—from your past that would most closely match the new situation. In the case of the shadow, the subconscious mind associates a previous image to evoke an emotion. That's why it's important that you try to surround yourself with an environment that can provide your subconscious with new associations, ones that work for you.

The simplest way to determine how your subconscious mind has affected you is to look at how it has affected your life so far. What habits do you have that are nonproductive? What beliefs do you hold that don't work in your current situation? Are you seeing spiders where there are only shadows?

Mind Has Dominance over Body

I made the point earlier that there is a connection between the mind and the body, that the subconscious mind controls the automatic functions of the body. Obviously the relationship is mutually beneficial, as neither can exist without the other. But in this relationship, the mind has dominance. All of the actions that you take—or more accurately, that your body takes—are due to the influence of your mind.

Consider this: your eyes don't see, your nose doesn't smell, your tongue doesn't taste. They are organs that transmit sensations to the brain, and your brain translates them into the color red, the smell of perfume, or the sweetness of honey. Your body is merely the conduit through which the world transmits itself.

We know that the brain is not the mind. The mind takes the sensory information provided to it by the brain and creates your reaction. If you enjoy the taste of honey, it's due to the pleasurable associations that your mind connects with that taste—not with the bees that produce the honey. Yet, guess how different your reaction would be if you were attacked by bees as a child! You would associate that bad experience with the honey. Different associations lead to different reactions.

The mind has dominance of the body because it controls your emotions. Your emotions affect your actions and reactions. Medical research long ago established the connection between your state of mind and your physical health. Physiological conditions such as the fight-or-flight response, with an increase in adrenaline due to perceived danger, are well established. Stressful conditions can cause an increase in blood pressure. Something as simple as a sad movie can cause you to cry—a physiological response to something your mind perceives.

A poor state of mind can actually cause illness. Researchers have found that depression can cause lowered immunity, making sufferers more susceptible to other diseases. Taken to another level, a poor state of mind often leads to reckless behavior, such as substance abuse or seeking dangerous situations. At its worst, the mind can cause the ultimate destructive behavior—suicide.

On the other hand, illness can also be fought off with the mind. Norman Cousins was an editor for the *New York Evening Post* and the *Saturday Review*. At one point Cousins was diagnosed with a debilitating form of arthritis that left him bedridden and in constant pain. Doctors were forced to give him large doses of painkillers to help relieve his suffering. As his condition worsened, he was told that he had little chance of surviving. Cousins decided to take his treatment into his own hands.

Cousins checked out of the hospital and into a hotel. He had read about the benefits of vitamin C, so he started taking large doses intravenously. Additionally, he began to read positive literature, filling his mind with messages of hope, faith, and love. He added laughter to his treatment by watching old Marx Brothers movies. Cousins recounted his experience in his book *Anatomy of an Illness*: "I made the joyous discovery that ten minutes of genuine belly laughter had an anesthetic effect and would give me at least two hours of pain-free sleep. When the pain-killing effect of the laughter wore off, we would switch on the motion picture projector again." Norman Cousins went on to live several years longer than his doctors had predicted.

As it turns out, Norman Cousins was a pioneer whose experience was backed up by later research. One study by Erik J. Giltay, PhD, of the Institute of Mental Health, in the February 27, 2006, issue of *Archives of Internal Medicine*, looked at the effects of the mind's power and its effect on more traditional diseases. The study concluded that "optimistic outlook may protect against coronary disease in older men."

In their book *Emotional Longevity*, Norman Anderson and Elizabeth Anderson tell how an optimistic outlook can not only lead to a longer life, but to a better quality of life. Optimists have lower blood pressure and heightened immunity. Asthmatics are able to breathe easier when they write down traumatic events that would normally cause a reaction. People that are in good relationships seem to have a higher resistance to everything from the common cold to heart disease.

In study after study, scientists are discovering that a person's attitude determines not only how long he or she lives, but also the quality of his or her physical health. The medical field's almost exclusive focus on the mechanics of the body ignores what some ancient cultures have always known—the mind controls the body's health.

Use Your Mind Power on Purpose

What caused the improvement in the physical health of Norman Cousins and others who have "thought" their way to better health? Their minds. They worked hard to manage their emotions so that their minds could work with their bodies to eliminate the causes of disease and to make them feel better. Norman Cousins used laughter to get rid of pain; others have reduced stress to beat a variety of conditions. In all cases, the patients have worked to communicate with their subconscious minds so that they had the best chance to feel well.

Just as the subconscious mind controls your physical health, it also controls your financial health, your emotional health, your career health, and the health of your relationships. Our attitudes and actions determine our results and our success.

For example, a seasoned, successful person has developed beliefs and habits in his subconscious. He calmly and efficiently performs the actions necessary to achieve success.

A rookie, on the other hand, has no such subconscious tools to call on for help. In the beginning every action is hit or miss, due to nervousness and inexperience. Consequently, the results are hit or miss.

Now we're getting to a really important point; in fact, it's what we've been building up to for the last two chapters.

As a human being, you have the ability to **mold** your subconscious mind into your greatest friend and supporter—an unbelievably strong ally that can serve you and do all the heavy lifting on the road to achieving your goals. When I spoke earlier of "changing the equation," this is what I meant. You can use your conscious mind to choose exactly what thoughts and feelings to feed your subconscious mind in order to develop it in the direction you want it to go. Read this paragraph again because this is how you command your future!

How do you feed your subconscious mind? You guide your subconscious by giving it the information you want it to have. The subconscious mind believes whatever it's told. If you (it) hear negativity all the time, it will act in such a way as to fulfill that negative image. If, on the other hand, you feed your subconscious a steady diet of positive messages—through visualization, reviewing your success goals, or using affirmations—then your subconscious will do all it can to take you in a positive direction.

This is how we install and maintain our success beliefs, habits, and paradigms.

This regular feeding of your subconscious mind is absolutely the most important step in achieving success. I call this your *Inner-Forming*¨, because it forms your mind—your "inside," if you will. It is absolutely critical work that never ends. When done properly (as I'll explain later), your Inner-Forming¨ cannot fail in producing the results that you want in your life.

In the coming chapters, I'm also going to discuss your behaviors and actions in the physical world (what I call *Outer-Performing*¨). These are important too, but because actions have their roots in the mind, the Inner-Forming¨ is always more important. The fact is, your Inner-Forming¨ will automatically add the right energy boost to your Outer-Performing¨.

At this point I hope you are beginning to get an idea of how much influence your subconscious mind has over your life and what might be possible if you can harness its energy. Remember that you have tremendous intellectual faculties at your disposal. As motivational author and speaker W. Clement Stone often said, "Whatever the mind of man can conceive and believe, it can achieve."

If the subconscious mind has so much control over your life, then clearly you will want to control your subconscious mind. The way you gain control of your life and your results (by controlling your mind) is through self-leadership.

4
Taking Command

I am the master of my fate:
I am the captain of my soul.

—William Ernest Henley

Up to now I've emphasized the massive effect and power your mind has on your life. You may have lived your life to this point with no idea that your past experiences had such a grip on you. With all the discussion about influences, patterns, and implanted suggestions, you may have started to feel as though someone else is controlling your brain. Actually, nothing could be further from the truth.

Your mind belongs to you. Your subconscious is not something alien, something separate from you. Your subconscious is you. True, it can be like having ownership of a feisty dog or an unbroken horse. The trick is to develop your mind to the point where it proves useful to you, functioning in the ways that will help you succeed.

What we're talking about here is *self-leadership*—asserting control over your own mind and actions, and reducing the influence that others have on you. Taking control of your life is not only a key to success, but also a definition for being a healthy adult. As long as you continue to hand the steering wheel of your life to another person (or institution), you can't really live a fulfilling life.

Self-leadership also means deciding to create a space where your conscious and subconscious minds can work together so you can control your life. Success is not guaranteed anywhere along the way in life, but you can put yourself into situations where the chances for success are far greater. When your conscious and subconscious work together via Inner-Forming˝ and Outer-Performing˝, you are applying the two most powerful forces in the universe.

Self-leadership is recognizing what you want out of life and demonstrating the maturity to resist being sidetracked by the nearest shiny object, or the latest idea to grab your attention. The statement "discover what you want out of life, then go after it" is so simple that it's almost a cliché. Nonetheless, almost no one lives their life in accordance with that philosophy. As simple as the statement is, the actual practice of it in daily life requires supreme self-leadership.

In our modern culture, the biggest obstacle we have is the number of choices we're offered. Distractions can pull us off-task in a second, and our senses are overloaded with offers. The media and society stimulate us without mercy, and it's often hard to decide what to do. Against all the stimuli, however, we have a secret weapon—choice.

Choosing Your Actions and Reactions

In his book, *The 7 Habits of Highly Effective People*, Stephen Covey discusses the gap between stimulus and response, between action and reaction. Normally, we are creatures forced to rely on stimulus/response. If you accidentally touch a hot stove (stimulus), you immediately jerk your hand away (response). The same pattern unfolds when, for example, someone speaks angrily to you. That's a stimulus that most of us respond to without thinking, usually in an angry manner of our own.

If we decide to be self-leaders, however, we take advantage of the gap between stimulus and response, and *choose* how we are going to react. We can take into consideration the specifics of the situation and decide what response will be most useful. In that way, we take control of our actions away from the other person and situation, and we assert our leadership by responding in a way that adds to our life rather than detracts from it.

Self-leadership is also recognizing that we have the power to change. What separates the human mind from animals is that we understand that what *is* now is not what *was* before, nor is it necessarily what *will be* later. The world changes, and human beings recognize that fact. What puts the leader a step above that level is understanding that the capacity for change lies within each of us. What you are now is not necessarily what you can be later.

Regardless of your circumstances, no matter how dire or desperate, you have the power to change at least one thing: your reaction to your circumstances. The innate essence of yourself cannot be touched by others if you don't allow it. People in the worst possible conditions have shown honor, integrity, and courage throughout their ordeals.

Viktor Frankl was a Jewish doctor who had a successful practice in Germany. During World War II he was rounded up with his family and shipped to a concentration camp. His entire family died in the camps, and Frankl was filled with despair. A specialist in neurology and psychiatry, Frankl saw others who were even more depressed than he was, to the point that they gave up and let themselves die.

Frankl determined that he would not die. He worked with his fellow prisoners to help them resist despondency and the desire to die. One day, finding himself worried over trivial details on how to get more food and less arduous work, Frankl became disgusted with himself and forced his thoughts to another matter. He imagined standing in front of a class, lecturing the students about the psychology of the concentration camp.

In that way, Frankl was able to rise above his situation and look on it as an experience that he and others could learn from. He took an objective view, with the determination that he would observe his situation without emotion, without suffering. By using this method, his harsh conditions were not able to affect his inner self, the essence of his humanity. Frankl decided that regardless of what injuries, pain, or indignities his guards might inflict on him, they could not touch that part of him that he controlled.

Very few people are subjected to the experiences that Frankl suffered. However, we can use his lesson to determine what we can do in our own lives. You have the choice. That realization is what gives you real power.

Power brings with it the willingness to do something about your choices. Once you realize that you are power-*full*, not power-*less*, you have an obligation to yourself to analyze the choices you make. Most of us spend our lives living according to the whims of circumstance and the wishes of other people. That's what brings unhappiness. When we use our power to change, we are on the road to true happiness and success.

The Decision

The realization that you have the power to change inevitably leads to the moment when you decide that you *will* change. That moment of decision is the turning point. When you have become so disgusted with your circumstances, or have developed such a hunger for improving your life that you will do anything to change, then you have made the Decision.

The Decision is vitally important in any attempt to change your life and be successful. The moment that you feel a deep, genuine commitment to changing your circumstances and controlling your life, you will be unstoppable. This moment can't be faked. It's a powerful moment of transformation for you. Your emotional junk bin is full, and you are refusing to load any more into it. My moment occurred while I was shivering in that freezing basement!

The moment of decision to take control of your life is a pivotal experience in self-leadership. Although you can—and should—write your thoughts down, this decision doesn't exist on paper. It only exists in your heart and in your gut. It's a moment of emotion, of passion, and, as we learned in the previous chapters, the subconscious mind communicates in emotions. You are communicating with your subconscious mind in its own language and telling it what you want it to do.

The Three Pillars of Self-Leadership

If you wanted to create a master plan for commanding and ruling your own future, it would contain three fundamental concepts—accountability, responsibility, and perseverance. If it were simply a matter of whipping up a batch of success and drinking it, life would be easy. Unfortunately, being human is hard. We are susceptible to moments of weakness and poor judgment. Even if you work hard to eradicate negative influences or patterns that are not useful, you're not guaranteed 100 percent success 100 percent of the time.

The amount of accountability, responsibility, or perseverance that you can demonstrate at any given time will wax and wane, sometimes at the worst possible moment. The good news is that you don't have to be perfect. Human frailty is something that even the greatest leaders and the most successful people in the world have to contend with. Somehow, despite their weaknesses, these leaders keep succeeding. If you find yourself in a bad moment, keep your chin up—you're in good company.

What exactly are these three miracle ingredients?

Accountability is when you decide that you are the one who put yourself in your present situation. There are no excuses and no blame. When you're a true self-leader, you quit giving yourself a built-in escape hatch. In today's society there are too many people who want to blame other people for their own poor decisions. Our current culture seems to cultivate a "victim mind-set," where it's always someone else's fault, regardless of how much we contributed to our own downfall. As a leader, you don't have this luxury.

Accountability means that you will take the consequences for your actions. When it comes time to answer for a situation, you will raise your hand. Not only do you cheat yourself when you let others take the blame for something you did, you also poison your relationships you have with other people. It takes moral courage to be accountable for your actions, a moral courage that most people rarely see. This moral courage is what enables you to achieve success.

Responsibility means that you make and keep promises, both to yourself and to others. Keeping promises and commitments is one of the most powerful tools that a successful person can implement. Again, our culture has made it acceptable—if not fashionable—for people to break promises.

You need only to read the newspaper to see examples of broken promises. Professional athletes want to "renegotiate" their contracts. Business executives are arrested for embezzling funds from their clients, shareholders, or employees. Politicians are notorious for making promises during a campaign, then reneging on them after the election.

On a more personal scale, think of the number of people who make appointments that they arrive late for, or even break. Look at deadlines for deliveries that were made, but missed. Some people are known for "always being late." These people show a lack of personal responsibility.

Make it a point from this point on to keep your promises. If you're unsure about your ability to fulfill a commitment, then don't make the commitment. A good rule of business conduct is to under-promise and over-deliver. In our culture we have become so jaded and inured to broken promises that a person who keeps his or her word stands out.

As you keep promises to other people, you become the one whom they can count on. That type of reputation is invaluable to a leader who wants to get things done. As you keep your promises, appointments, and commitments to others, you will find that they will keep their commitments to you more and more. Not only are you demonstrating self-leadership but you become an example and a leader to others.

Keeping promises to yourself is just as important as keeping promises to others. To achieve more, you have to develop successful habits. You develop these habits by getting into daily routines that develop you in ways you may have ignored before. We'll discuss exactly how to do this later when we cover Outer-Performing¯. It may be to start exercising regularly, or to write in a daily journal. Whatever it is, you have to make a commitment to work on these areas at specific times on a regular basis so that they become a habit.

Especially when you're first starting out, you will meet resistance. Other things become suddenly more urgent, and you find that you simply *must* take care of them first. At least, that's the rationalization that will present itself. If you make a promise to yourself that no matter what, you keep your commitment, then you will soon find that doing those things becomes habit.

One psychological aspect of keeping promises to yourself is that achieving success becomes more real to you. "If I can do this," you reason, "then maybe I can really succeed." Most of us are in the habit of putting promises to ourselves low on the list of priorities, when in reality there is nothing more important.

Results matter. Responsibility also means, to rephrase a famous slogan, just doing it. Someone once said that 90 percent of success is simply showing up. Although simplistic, the idea behind it contains a kernel of real truth. As a minimum, simply doing the things that are expected of you is one way to get ahead of almost everyone else. Always strive for the best possible result, doing the best work that you are capable of. Taking care of your business prevents logjams and delays further along your road to success.

Perseverance is sticking with your course of action regardless of how difficult it is. As I mentioned a few pages back, being a human being is tough. As hard as it is now, however, it's nothing compared to what the early settlers and pioneers of North America had to go through. Imagine if you had to travel across the North American continent in a wagon drawn by mules or oxen, suffering in freezing cold and debilitating heat. It puts having to wait on an elevator in perspective, doesn't it?

Of course, we have to contend with things that earlier peoples didn't have to worry about. The enormous number of social interactions we have to go through on a daily basis is staggering. We have to count on other people for many of our needs, and each one of those people is capable of disappointing us—broken promises, lies, backstabbing, and other negative qualities are too often part of the equation when dealing with people.

Perseverance means accepting that there will be hardships but pressing on anyway. If you can't accomplish your task one way, find another. Most of what we consider problems are actually inconveniences. You have tremendous resources at your disposal if you only look for them. Demonstrating perseverance means that you don't let the closure of one avenue prevent you from achieving your goals.

One thing that perseverance does *not* mean is compromising your values. Sure, there are shortcuts and easier ways to get some things done, but if you feel that you have to violate your ethics to accomplish a goal then you haven't looked hard enough. We face almost unbearable pressure to cut corners or cheat to get things done. Doing the right thing is always harder than cheating, but if you start down the road to unethical behavior, then you are violating a promise to yourself—the promise to align your actions with your values.

Years ago I had a friend whose father was the president and owner of a midsize manufacturing company. He gave me a middle management position. My job was to manage people who were much older than I was and who had been with the company much longer.

Needless to say, there was some resentment when I came in "off the street" to be their boss. I didn't have any knowledge of the business either, but I believed in my ability as a manager, and I had confidence that over time the relationship with my employees would become a good working relationship.

Every day, every hour, and almost every minute I had to be persistent in proving myself to them and changing their minds about me. I had to gently confront them sometimes when they were being unfair with me, and I had to behave properly every moment to gain their confidence and bring forth the good working relationship that I envisioned. It took a long time, but through persistence, I accomplished my goal, and years later when I left the company my workers were really sad to see me go.

Of the three variables, perseverance may be the most important. As Calvin Coolidge once said, "Nothing in the world can take the place of persistence. Talent will not; nothing in the world is more common than unsuccessful men with talent. Genius will not; unrewarded genius is almost a proverb. Education will not; the world is full of educated derelicts. Persistence and determination alone are omnipotent."

These three fundamentals—accountability, responsibility and perseverance—are vitally important to your ability to create and live your dream. So what exactly is your dream? Your journey of achieving what you want actually begins by describing the destination.

5

Your Future, Your Choice

The greater danger for most of us is not that our aim is too high and we miss it, but that it is too low and we reach it.

—Michelangelo

Successful people see things that don't exist. Normally when you see things that don't exist, people think you're crazy. Though, what successful people see that others don't is a vision of what success would look like. Successful people have the power to look beyond what is available to them at this moment and to envision what they will look like when they have reached their goals.

Vision is what separates mere managers from true leaders. Many of the greatest leaders in history have been visionaries. Mahatma Gandhi saw an India where the people ruled themselves. Henry Ford envisioned a world where everyone drove his horseless carriage. Ray Kroc saw an America where millions of people ate hamburgers at his drive-in restaurants. All of these visionaries were told by those around them that they were crazy because they saw things that didn't exist—yet. It was only with their crystal-clear vision that they were able to create the very things that they first imagined.

A true vision is a static image. It's a picture of what you want to do, what you want to be, what you want to have, what you want to create. It's a snapshot of the perfect situation that you want to work for; maybe it's you shaking the hand of a customer you just made a sale to. Maybe it's a picture of you receiving a reward for services that you've provided to the community. Maybe you see yourself walking across the stage to receive a diploma as you receive a degree.

In all these cases, you should have felt the emotions that are important to you—positive emotions that you can associate with the feeling of success. As you envision this future that you want to create, you should either feel pride, a sense of accomplishment, or some other positive emotion. Your positive emotion will drive you to want to create a physical version of the very vision that you see in your mind's eye.

The image that you see should be the ultimate goal that you're striving for. It's important that you create as sharp and clear an image as possible when you envision your success—the clearer the vision, the clearer the path. When the world throws obstacles in your way and you have to solve problems and take care of issues that you never anticipated, always keep this vision in front of you. That way you'll find the drive deep inside yourself that will carry you through to the next step of achieving your goal.

Think about jigsaw puzzles. Have you ever bought a 1,000-piece jigsaw puzzle and tried to put it together without looking at the picture on the box? Without an image to work toward, you don't know if the blue pieces are sky, water, a house, a balloon, or what. Expert puzzle solvers may be able to reconstruct a puzzle with nothing to go on, but think how much easier it is when you look at the box and can see what you're shooting for.

Success in life is much more complicated than a jigsaw puzzle. Like a puzzle, however, the journey toward success has pieces that fit together and a logic to achieving the end result. And like a jigsaw puzzle, it's much easier to reach your goal when you have a clear picture in mind before you start.

The difference between a jigsaw puzzle and real life is that when you are creating a vision in real life, you're imagining something that doesn't exist yet. You're creating an imaginary future reality based on nothing more than your dreams and desires. By creating a concrete image of your future, you are giving your subconscious mind the instructions it needs to help you create a future. The associated emotions that go along with that image are what will keep you going when you're confronted with obstacles.

Develop Your Vision

You may be asking yourself, "how do I develop a vision?" The easiest way is to ask yourself questions; Tony Robbins, as I quoted previously, always recommends asking high-quality questions, and it's the answer to those questions that will determine what kind of goals you set for yourself. You may ask questions such as "if time and money were no object, what would it be possible for me to do?"

Many times we are busy working through the day, trying to find answers that we don't need. If you're asking yourself the wrong questions, then it's impossible for you to find the correct answers. This is when it's time for you to consider your priorities and to determine what is really important to you.

The correct questions to ask yourself are not necessarily the first ones that you think of. You need time for introspection, contemplation, and to ask yourself questions about the things that are most important to you. As I mentioned in chapter one, we all have different roles in our lives—different parts that we play in our different categories, whether it's our personal lives, our professional lives, or our community. Each of these roles will require different questions, and each of those questions will require different answers. The things that are important to you in your professional life aren't—or shouldn't be—as important to you as the answers to questions you have in your personal life.

In each of the categories or roles that you ask questions, you will want to come up with answers that greatly excite you, but that scare you a bit, too. When you ask your questions, you can't put limits on what you're looking for. What you're looking for is the end result of a long process. But at this point, you don't think about the process. You think about what you want.

Generally, you will see certain things easier than others. When you create your picture, you'll see some items very clearly and in great detail. Those are the ones that you normally need to work toward. Your subconscious mind has worked on these goals and visions without you realizing it. When you can see a new car, notice the bright, shiny color. See the sunlight glistening off the glass. Then you're well on your way to creating the image that will help compose your vision. That's only one simple example, but you will have other vivid images in each of the roles that you play.

The purpose for creating this vision is to evoke the emotion that accompanies it. That emotion is how you communicate to your subconscious that such a goal is possible. You're creating a new reality for your subconscious mind to grasp. When your subconscious mind sees the vivid image, it will automatically start working on ways to help you reach that goal.

The emotion that you have created for your subconscious mind is the Decision. Making the sincere decision that you're going to work toward a particular goal is the key moment at which you will actually start achieving that goal. Whether it's to lose 20 pounds, reach a new sales figure, or some other goal, that decisive moment is when you will achieve the sense of purpose necessary for you to be able to reach your final vision.

You may feel the intense emotion that you were meant to do something special with your life. That you were meant to do and be more than you are now. That emotion, so common in ambitious people, can cause huge amounts of frustration and inner turmoil if it's not directed. However, once you have that vision, all that potential is aimed at achieving your one vivid image. Instead of eating away inside you, your energy creates a sense of fulfillment and accomplishment as you put it to use in your quest for success.

When we think about successful people in history, we particularly make heroes of those who have shown great devotion to a single cause. We think about those men and women who have devoted their lives to a vision, who had the drive to overcome obstacles and to achieve greatness, despite everything that was put in their way. We don't remember them for their faults or their failures, but for the particular successes that they had. The great people in history are the ones who had a vision.

Years ago when I began what turned out to be a four-year stint in the music business, I had a dream of producing a complete CD on my own. I knew that one day I would control the entire process: creating the music and also the final product. While I was living in New York City and working in the recording studios, I deliberately learned every single step involved with engineering and producing a music CD. I learned from all the experienced professionals in the industry so that I would be ready when my chance came.

After several years of doing this, I was armed with the knowledge and experience that I needed. I began to have fun producing bands on the side. Working with a band from the very beginning to the end is quite an experience. There are so many people and so many things involved that, although it was challenging, it was very rewarding to be able to finally create the finished product.

I could never have reached this level without the vision of seeing myself producing a band's music from start to finish. There were many long days and nights when it would've been much easier for me to go home and get some rest. Instead, I was able to learn from others and develop the skills I needed to reach my goal. It was this vision that gave me the drive and the sense of purpose I needed to reach the ultimate goal: producing music and creating CDs.

Drive and Passion

When people can sense drive and passion in an individual, they respect it. When you read biographies of great people, their biographers always emphasize the drive and singleness of purpose that drove the individual to great accomplishment. People applaud drive. They respect passion.

Why is passion important? Because passion is energy. Passion is what makes creation possible and makes achieving great things real. Passion is the fire in the belly that everyone needs in order to reach their full potential. Halfhearted efforts are almost always doomed to fail. It's only when there is passion and excitement about a project that things get done.

Passion helps create the sense of urgency that makes us want to get things done today and not wait until tomorrow. It's easy to want to maintain the status quo, to avoid doing anything that requires effort or energy. A sense of urgency is what we need to get things done today, right now. If we wait until the time is right, we will be waiting forever because the time is never "right" to do something that has never been done before.

It should be clear by now that no one ever succeeds alone. We all depend upon the help of other people at some point in our journey. When you have passion, it excites others who can help. That excitement about a project or a mission is contagious—passion feeds on itself. Their excitement, in turn, reinforces our passion and our sense of purpose and ultimately helps us create the reality of our vision.

Passion also helps us push through troubles and disappointments. Consider men like Gandhi or Martin Luther King Jr. and the people that worked with them, who suffered not only disappointments but humiliation and physical punishment. Yet their passion found its way into the hearts of others, and ultimately the visions of both these men were realized.

Most of the obstacles that we encounter are small compared to those suffered by Gandhi or King. Our problems are usually much more mundane and involve situations that are nowhere near life-and-death. However, the same drive that those men used to get them through their tribulations can help you work your way past any obstacles that present themselves. Your passion, drive, and emotion are there to help you achieve your goal.

At this point you may be wondering, "How do I develop such passion? How can I feel such emotion for my goal and my vision?" First of all, you need to remember the emotion that your vision evoked, and of course, your vision should have been something that you're passionate about. Many of us try to suppress our emotions. Our culture, our family, and our environment often teach us that the expression of emotions is improper.

For you to achieve your goal, however, it's important that you remember the emotion that you felt when you imagined the future reality that you are trying to create. Turning that emotion into positive energy is the key to developing your sense of purpose and also to maintaining the drive necessary for you to be able to achieve your goal.

Another way to develop passion about your vision and your goal is to find something that is representative of the goal. For example, your goal may be to earn more money in the coming year. To represent that goal, you might have a photograph of a beautiful new sports car on your desk or wall. That photograph is a concrete image of what having more money can represent to you. Find a symbol that vividly represents what you're trying to achieve. When people ask you what you're working so hard for, point to the picture.

You can also immerse yourself in the subject of your goal. If you're working very hard and the payoff will be a trip to Europe, then find out everything you can about the countries that you'll visit. Learn to speak the languages. Find out about the history and architecture and the customs of the people. By immersing yourself in the details of your trip, you will feed the passion that drives you to do the extra work necessary to reach your goal. Do this with the details of your particular goal. Wallow in the subjects of your goal and you will discover that the vision seems even more within your grasp.

During this time it's also important to engage your senses as completely as possible. Use concrete imagery to create a vivid picture of your goal. *Smell* the aroma of the leather seats in your new car. *Listen* to the ruffle of the bills as you handle a stack of cash. *Feel* the texture of the wood grain on the new desk you bought for your office. Experiencing these details in advance is actually an important part of your Inner-Forming˜, which we'll discuss in more depth later.

Your subconscious mind doesn't have a filter when it receives messages. It simply takes as real whatever sensory information you give it. Most of the time these messages are incidental, coming from whatever happens to occur at any given time. Now, though, when it comes to your goal, you are taking control of the information your subconscious mind receives. Whatever sensory details work the best for you, use them. This is a highly personal process because only you can determine what details are most vivid for yourself.

Even if it seems silly, use the information that is meaningful to you. One acquaintance of mine had grown up in a small town where the wealthiest man wore a pinkie ring with an enormous gemstone in it. Although as a grown man he was not particularly fond of jewelry, he equated the concept of wealth with wearing such a ring. When he imagined earning large amounts of money, he used that ring from his childhood as a symbol of what he could afford to buy after he reached his goal. Whether he actually bought the ring or not was immaterial—the image of it represented the type of wealth he wanted to earn.

Creating Goal Statements

What your conscious mind needs is a tool that can demonstrate precisely how you are going to accomplish your goals. There comes a time when preparation stops and action begins. You want your actions to be intelligent and directed at achieving your success. The most effective way to reach your goals is through effectively setting goals.

Effective goals have attributes that have been proven to work. There is no benefit, moral or otherwise, in expending time and energy on techniques and activities that don't accomplish your goals. By setting goals with a system that has been shown to work, you can reach your goals in the most direct way.

First of all, it's vital that your goals be *worthy* of your values. An old saying says that the ends justify the means—essentially rationalizing any actions along the way. I believe that if a goal (the ends) has to be reached by disreputable methods, then it is not a goal worth pursuing. Goals can still be ambitious and advantageous for you without injuring others. On the reverse, by helping yourself in a moral and ethical way, you will benefit others.

By keeping in mind the underlying idea that your goals must be worthy, you can construct goals that meet the following proven criteria: a goal must be *specific*, have a *time frame*, be *achievable*, be *measurable*, and must be a *priority*.

A *specific* goal is one that differentiates itself from other goals. You may want to earn more money and to lose weight. Those would be two specific goals. You have already started being specific when you created the vivid image for your vision. You may envision yourself running a marathon—that's a specific goal. You may see yourself driving a new car—that's a specific goal.

Having specific goals solidifies them in your subconscious mind. How much more money do you want to earn? A specific goal would be, "I want to earn $100,000 a year." Another would be, "I want to lose 20 pounds." When you're specific with your goal, you can point at it after you reach it and tell yourself, "I did it."

The *time frame* is important because it lights a fire under you. The whole point of setting a goal is to eventually reach it. Without a time frame, it's not a goal—it's a wish. You've probably heard someone say, "I really want to lose some weight someday," or, "I need to quit smoking someday." As you already know, *someday* never comes. It's a moving target on the horizon, always retreating.

In the example above, you might set a goal of earning $100,000 *by the end of next year*. "I want to save $5000 within six months" is also a good example of a time frame. Using the commonly accepted idea that healthy weight loss should be no more than one to two pounds a week, you could say, "I want to lose 20 pounds within 15 weeks." Always be intelligent and realistic about your time frames, and then stick to them.

Goals must also be *achievable*—that is, they must be something you can reach with your own efforts. Earning more money is achievable, winning the lottery is not. If you are trusting in luck and chance to reach your goals, then you are not attracting into your life what is needed to achieve your goals. A definition that I love is the one of *luck*—when preparation meets opportunity. In other words, you make your own luck.

What you will discover as you become more prepared (through working toward your goals) is that you become luckier. Opportunities will start to come your way. As you take the actions necessary to reach your goals, your eyes will become more open to the unlimited potential you possess. It begins, however, with setting a goal that you achieve through your own efforts.

Your goal should also be *measurable*. As with specificity, when you reach your goal, you should be able to confidently say, "I did it." By making your goal something measurable, you can accurately track your progress as you go along. Using measurements ensures that you can determine if you are on track or not. If your goal is to lose 20 pounds within 15 weeks, you don't want to wait until the end of the time frame to determine if you've reached your goal or not. Monitoring your progress is vital to reaching a goal because if a particular course of action is not working, it can be adjusted or abandoned for another that is more effective.

It's also important that your goal be a *priority*. You can set goals in every aspect of your life—in fact, it's a good idea to do so. However, make sure that your secondary goals are not hindering your more important goals. You may have a goal of saving more money, but also have a goal of upgrading your wardrobe. Determine which of these goals is more important. Then find a way to fit the secondary goal within the high-priority one or abandon the secondary goal.

When you've completed your goal-setting process, you should be able to create a goal statement. Use the following principles to create effective goal statements. Write down

- Your specific goal in crystal clear terms

- The definite date by which you intend to achieve your goal

- A definite plan for achieving your goal

Take special care to create a goal statement for yourself that really excites you and be sure to write it in the present tense. Read your goal statement in the morning and at night, making sure that you see, feel, and believe yourself having already achieved your goal.

Reading your goal statement twice a day in this manner is a powerful piece of Inner-Forming". Each time you review your statement, you are constructing your future, brick by brick. The repeated recitation of your goal creates an image of your success framed in the present tense. This forms a tidal wave in your subconscious mind, moving all its energy toward the fulfillment of your goal.

Because of the nature of the subconscious mind, you are literally commanding your future when you read your goal statement and see and feel your success.

Subgoals

As you work toward each goal, you will likely need to set various subgoals. These are the stepping-stones you will need to reach your ultimate goal. Set these subgoals the same way you set your larger goal, by being specific, using a time frame, etc., then create as many subgoals as you need to reach your objective. Some goals will need more subgoals than others. That's okay. Take as many steps as you need—no one will be grading you on this. You only grade yourself after you reach your ultimate goal.

Write out your goal statement. When you see the process in concrete form, it takes on a new reality, one in which your goal appears not only possible, but plausible. Keep your goals handy and look at them often. Each day check to see if there is a step you can take that will lead you closer to your goal.

Vision, passion, goals—these are the ingredients you need to add great force to reaching the success you desire and deserve. These elements release your energy and remove the shackles that you place on yourself.

But to maximize your effectiveness in achieving your goals, it's important that you have a winning strategy. That's the subject of the next chapter.

6

A Winning Strategy

What's the use of running
if you are not on the right road?

—German proverb

Leonardo da Vinci was arguably one of the most intelligent men who ever lived. Besides his famous artwork (*Mona Lisa*, *The Last Supper*), da Vinci developed inventions and ideas for inventions that were far ahead of his time. One of the most fascinating pieces of writing ever created is da Vinci's journal. He used a combination of words and images to work out ideas on paper before he committed to them in the physical world. In that same way, you will need to figure out what approach to take before you actually start the steps to achieving your goal.

In chapter three we looked at the concept that there are two creations for any action. First comes the mental creation, which is a vision or a concept that is imagined in the conscious mind. Second, the actual creation of your mental image comes into the real world. In this chapter we will begin discussing the way to make the transition from the mental creation to the actual physical creation.

Whether your creation is something concrete (like constructing a building or painting a portrait) or something more intangible (like building your relationship with your child), you must have a method you can use to transfer that mental image into the real world. This process is well-known but extremely crucial; it is where the rubber meets the road.

The world has great respect for a person who can get things done. Although there are many ways to get things done, what's the best way? In most cases, of course, there are many different ways to accomplish a task. Some ways are harder, and some are easier. What we are looking for is the most effective way to accomplish particular tasks. To accomplish anything in an effective manner requires a strategy.

Many people often misunderstand the meaning of the word *strategy*. Using strategy simply means giving a matter some thought before you enter into action. There is nothing particularly mysterious or devious about thinking before you act. The most successful people are those who don't waste energy on doing things the hard way— unless the hard way is the most effective.

To get things done in the most effective way requires a proper mind-set. As we have already seen, there are too many times when we believe that we are using the most effective strategy simply because that's what we've been told or led to believe. "We've always done it that way" is a great indicator that a strategy needs analysis. You need to analyze the strategies that you have used in the past to determine if they have been effective. Did you achieve the results that you wanted in the most efficient way?

Your Outlook

Before you can develop a strategy, however, you have to look within yourself to determine if you have the proper *outlook*. What is an outlook? It is simply a philosophy of life, the lens that you look through to see the world. For example, people who feel that they have been victims their entire lives tend to have a more negative view of the world, believing that the world owes them something. What you're looking for is the most effective outlook to help you realize your visions. Truly successful people have a particular outlook, and the best way to be successful is to do what other successful people do.

There are different kinds of outlooks. First, there is the *nothing outlook*—a view of life where the person chooses not to participate. A person with a nothing outlook doesn't need to worry about a strategy because they are not doing anything anyway. These people have decided to let things happen to them rather than trying to make things happen. They simply go with the flow so that they don't have to become involved. Needless to say, very few successful people have this kind of outlook.

Another outlook is the all-too-common *competitive-destructive outlook*. This type of outlook is very aggressive and is carried by people who hold a very hostile view of the world. No one who has any sort of lasting success has this type of outlook. We'll go into more detail about the competitive-destructive outlook shortly.

Related to the competitive-destructive outlook is the *scarcity mentality*. This mentality views the world as zero-sum. Every accomplishment, achievement, award, or reward must be taken from someone else. This mentality is often held by people who have been raised in a very aggressive, anarchistic environment.

Another outlook is the *creative-cooperative outlook*. This type of outlook is the one most often held by those who have achieved lasting success. The creative-cooperative outlook is one that capitalizes on the concept of abundance.

The particular outlook you choose to view the world through is closely related to your values. Having good values equates to having a good outlook. If you'll remember, I have placed a lot of emphasis so far on choosing values that would be beneficial to the world. Good values, besides exhibiting a generosity of spirit, are simply more effective. If your goal is to achieve success with the added help of other people, then having good values, and therefore a good outlook, simply works better.

Competitive-Destructive Outlook

The competitive-destructive outlook—for simplicity's sake let's call it the *C-D outlook*—is used by people who harbor a grudge or hostility toward the world: "I'm going to get mine regardless of the cost to other people." This type of outlook is based on the scarcity mentality, where there have to be winners and losers in every transaction. If you win, then I lose, so I must win to avoid losing.

The C-D outlook is characterized by feelings of jealousy and envy. The success of another person creates turmoil for someone who holds the C-D outlook. They feel resentment for anyone who is more successful, who is better looking, who has more money, or anyone who they feel has some sort of advantage. These are the people who feel that all rich people—not a few, not some, but *all*—attained their wealth by exploiting or stealing from others. With that view, how do you think the person with a C-D outlook will try to attain his own wealth?

The problem with the C-D outlook is that it is not useful for achieving lasting success because it focuses on other people rather than the goal. The subconscious mind is preoccupied with the wrong image. Of course, there are actual examples of people who have achieved faux success by nefarious means. These are the ones who have a particular God-given talent in a particular area that they exploit to gain wealth. And their downfall is all too common.

Think of the number of professional athletes who have lived lifestyles that destroyed their careers and eventually left them penniless, in poor health, and often with legal troubles. Deep down these athletes knew that what they were using as a "strategy" was nothing more than carrying over a mind-set that they learned earlier in their lives. They surrounded themselves not with people who could help them and improve their lives, but with those of similar outlooks. An entourage of gold diggers and parasites may boost your ego for a while, but when the gold is gone, so is the entourage.

Mike Tyson was one of the most feared men in heavyweight boxing in the 1980s and 90s. He came from a troubled childhood, and a chance meeting with a trainer, Cus D'Amato, who showed him how to channel his aggression into the boxing ring led him to tremendous success in the sport. D'Amato was a father figure to Tyson, serving as his boxing manager and trainer as Tyson became successful. Mike Tyson became the youngest man ever to win the world heavyweight boxing title. After D'Amato's death, Kevin Rooney took over Tyson's training, doing all he could to keep Tyson focused despite Tyson's personal problems.

Eventually, though, Tyson's outlook drew a group of people around him who didn't care about him as a person, people who only wanted to use Tyson for their own gain. Tyson fired Rooney, and his downfall began. After a short time he lost the heavyweight title, was charged with various crimes, and ended his career disgraced and penniless. His outlook—despite tremendous physical talents—took away everything he had achieved. Tyson focused on short-term gain rather than a healthier life.

Attaining short-term gain is one of the pitfalls of the C-D outlook; a person only sees the bottom line as most important, and he or she tries to make all they can in a short amount of time. The short-term gain is characterized by greed as a core value—and greed as a value doesn't work. When you sacrifice long-term physical, emotional, or mental health for profit, you eventually lose all of it.

Look at the state of the American financial system today. Some greedy executives cheated shareholders, customers, and the system by misstating profits and benefits. They engaged in illegal and unethical practices, racking up millions of dollars in personal wealth, but their greed eventually caught up with them and the entire house of cards collapsed around them. Of course, not *all* executives achieved their success this way. You can't paint an entire class of people with the same brush.

The most time that any of us has on earth is a very brief period. Compared to the age of the Earth, one person's life is less than the blink of an eye. Don't waste the little time you have by trying to conquer everyone you know simply to gain earthly wealth or recognition. The best anyone can do is try to build something that will outlast his or her tiny lifespan. Expending all your effort in tearing down other's accomplishments doesn't build you up—it leaves only piles of rubble.

The question that arises, then, is "Is competition ever good?" The surprising answer is yes. Competition without destruction can be viewed as play or as sport. A spirit of competition can whet the appetite, add drive to achieving your goals, and force you to accomplish more than you thought possible. Of course, such a spirit can't be held by anyone with a negative outlook. Competition is a mechanism in the human mind that makes us work harder and longer than we thought we could. With the right mind-set, competition helps everyone achieve more—each person has his or her eye on the prize.

Competition can also help you pinpoint your weaknesses and eliminate them. Boxers soon find out if they are holding their hands too low—they get punched in the face! Likewise, businesses find out if their products are overpriced or if they have a product that is not as reliable as that of their competitors. Competition helps you discover your soft spots.

Once you have discovered your weaknesses, then the next step is to eliminate them. Competition can motivate you to find better, more efficient ways to reach success. Sales contests pit salespeople against one another, and many of these salespeople discover better ways to sell their products. What's great about such a contest is that the salespeople can use the tactics they discovered during the contest afterward to improve their sales.

Creative-Cooperative Outlook

The benefits of competition are only useful to those who have the creative-cooperative outlook (C-C outlook). Instead of resenting the winners, even those players who don't win a particular contest understand that they have gained lasting benefits. Instead of destruction, they have gained new ideas of creation. The C-C person has created a new way of reaching success by eliminating limited thinking. If everyone takes away this lesson from a competition, then everyone wins.

Building something is the essence of the C-C outlook. The best that any of us can hope for in life is to build a legacy that will outlive us. We do this by working with others to help everyone achieve his or her goals. The C-C outlook is characterized by sharing and caring. Very few people are architects of physical buildings, but every person is an architect of his or her own life. You can build something with your life that you can leave to your children, your friends, and those around you.

The C-C outlook is a display of the *abundance mentality*. The abundance mentality recognizes that the world—as far as human beings are concerned—is limitless. There are plenty of riches, either material or spiritual, for everyone. Each person can have a piece of the pie, and if we look hard, we can see that the pie gets bigger each time we achieve success that is in line with our values.

This key concept to the abundance mentality is recognized by anyone who has achieved lasting success. Look at the number of billionaires who have started programs or foundations to help others. There is a balance in the universe that determines whether you are worthy of having the success you work so hard to attain. Those with the abundance mentality know that universal law can't be broken—you can only break yourself against it.

On a more mundane level, the C-C outlook is simply more fun. People who are working together to achieve something great enter each day with a joyous, even laughing, demeanor. When obstacles present themselves and progress is harder to make, those with the C-C outlook know that they are not in the struggle alone and can enjoy the fellowship of their partners. Sharing hard work and completing difficult tasks bring people together in ways that are unknown to those who always want to take the easy way to success.

The abundance mentality is the opposite of the scarcity mentality. Working with others to achieve a goal creates a synergy that makes the impossible possible. What those with an abundance mentality find is that sometimes the whole is greater than the sum of its parts—that is, a team can accomplish more working together than what each member could achieve on his own.

President John F. Kennedy once said, "The rising tide lifts all boats." He used the term to defend his tax policies, but the point is the same for those who work with others. Shared success benefits everyone, and a higher level of success means greater success for all involved. This is why a loner who believes that he or she can only achieve success by himself misses out on true achievement. By helping others achieve their own dreams and goals, you gain when they do.

While on the topic of the most effective strategies and qualities needed for success, we must not leave out the important topic of integrity.

Integrity

If you go to a cemetery and look at a headstone, you'll probably see the date of birth and the date of death connected by a dash. When you realize the dash represents an entire life, it helps you focus on what you make of your own life. In *The 7 Habits of Highly Effective People*, Stephen Covey discusses an exercise in which you imagine your funeral. At that funeral, different people in your life stand up and describe what kind of person you were.

The point of Covey's exercise is to make you focus on the end result of your life. How do you want to be remembered by those closest to you? The quality of your memory depends on the relationships that you establish while you are alive. The quality of the life you live depends on your relationships with other people.

For a moment, think again of the many different roles you will play throughout your life, such as parent, sibling, child, coach, club member, or church member. The list is endless because of the complexity of our lives. However, a single thread runs through all these relationships—the importance of integrity.

Dictionary.com defines *integrity* as "adherence to moral and ethical principles." There can be no denying the fact that we each have principles that we follow, for good or for bad. The second definition for integrity, however, is intriguing: "the state of being whole and undiminished." For example, a king might fight to preserve the integrity of his kingdom.

Without the first definition of integrity you can't maintain the second definition. That is, your life cannot be considered whole unless you have established a set of principles to follow. A complete person cannot live his or her life without guidance of some type. Unless they have a set of values or a code that they follow, people will have an empty place within them.

Others can sense the empty place inside you, and it will affect your relationships. For example, if you don't value honesty, then others will sense that about you and will never fully trust anything you say. That lack of trust will affect every decision they make in their dealings with you.

There's an aphorism I heard once that says, "You know what you call someone who tells the truth 90 percent of the time? A *liar.*" This adage illustrates the importance of consistency in your actions. If you behave in a certain way most of the time, then occasions when you act outside your normal manner will stand out in people's minds, and this rare occurrence will be the perception they remember about you. Even though most of the time you tell the truth, people will consider you as untrustworthy because of any exceptions.

What this means is that the principles that you choose to follow are important. When you rely on basic principles, you develop a consistency in your actions, values, methods, measures, expectation, and outcomes. The degree to which you behave consistently is what determines what kind of person you are and what kind of person other people think you are.

What's more, human beings are unable to believe two principles that oppose each other, so you won't be able to justify actions inconsistent with one principle by citing another. That's why it's important that our principles be fundamental and able to adapt to a variety of situations.

For example, when delineating your principles, you might say that you always answer questions directly and truthfully. In some cases, as when dealing with another person's feelings, perhaps it might be better to skirt a direct question in such a way that you both preserve the person's feelings and avoid lying to them. A better-declared principle might be that you always tell the truth. In that way, your concern and compassion for other people does not conflict with your desire to be honest and forthright.

Carter's Rules for Integrity

In his book *Integrity*, Stephen L. Carter proposes three conditions that a person must meet in order to act with integrity. The first condition states that a person must be able and willing to discern what is right and what is wrong. The ability to make this judgment is a combination of all the factors that we've discussed previously (e.g., your childhood, your closest friends and relatives, the influence of different factors in society). For those who believe that "anything goes" or "the ends justify the means," there can be no room for integrity, as their behavior will vary according to the situation. They are not able to tell right from wrong other than as it suits their needs at the time.

For the second condition, Carter says that displaying integrity means acting on what you have discerned as right or wrong, even at personal cost. As I have emphasized throughout this book, the actions you take are the outer expression of your inner self. Others judge you by what they observe and perceive; actually living your life in a way consistent with your proclaimed beliefs is the only way they can make an accurate judgment. You may "talk the talk," but unless you "walk the walk," others may still have doubts or reservations about your integrity.

The idea of acting on your beliefs even when it may be to your temporary disadvantage seems self-defeating. It may *seem* that way, but, of course, what you are really doing is demonstrating that your integrity does not stem from self-interest or egoism, but rather from recognizing that being a complete person means your actions must correlate with your fundamental principles. Every time you adhere to your beliefs, you are keeping a promise to yourself.

A secondary benefit—but *only* a secondary benefit—is that when you act in a way that is right, even when it costs you personally, it proves to others that your integrity does not depend on personal gain. Your consistency lets others know that they can count on you without reservation. This sense of security infuses fresh air into a relationship, allowing open communication and expression that makes greater things possible.

Carter's third condition in demonstrating integrity states that you say openly that you are acting on your understanding of right from wrong. Because conducting oneself with integrity is relatively rare in today's dog-eat-dog culture, when you behave in a certain way most people will automatically interpret your actions as meaning that you will personally profit from your move.

In a sense, that judgment is accurate in fact but wrong in scope. Your benefit derives from your building yourself into a better person. This is a long-term profit, very different from what observers may think. Every act you take builds you as a person, contributing to your success by solidifying your inner self.

However, openly declaring that you are acting on your sense of right indicates to others that you are operating at a higher level. The first time someone hears you explain your actions in terms of right and wrong, they may have trouble believing you because so few people operate that way. Each subsequent time it happens, however, your credibility will grow. Eventually anyone who deals with you will understand your stance.

By no means am I saying that Carter's three conditions for integrity are the only ones. However, if you decide to maximize your relationships by demonstrating integrity, infusing every aspect of your life with the philosophy of conducting yourself honorably, then you are maximizing your chances of success in life. Not only will you go further, but you will also enjoy a higher quality of life.

When it comes time for your friends and family to describe your life, what will you want them to say? The dash between your birth date and death date—your life—is the only part of that situation you can control.

Specifically within your control are your outlook and your integrity. With an effective outlook and effective integrity, you'll be able to create a winning strategy to manifest your goals in physical reality.

The bedrock of your strategy will be your Inner-Forming˝. After all this talk of the absolute necessity and miraculous power of Inner-Forming˝, let's discuss several types for you to choose from and use.

7

Inner-Forming™

Victorious warriors win first and then go to war,
while defeated warriors go to war first and then seek to win.

—Sun Tzu

Most people would agree that it would be ridiculous to try to build a house starting with the roof. There would be nothing to hold it up—not even starting with the rafters to support it would work. No, we all agree that you have to begin with the foundation, the solid base that the entire structure rests upon. Because of gravity, we have to build a structure from the bottom up.

In the same way, any real change that you want to effect in your life has to comply with this principle. Change begins with establishing a foundation, something that everything else can sit upon. I call this foundation *Inner-Forming*˝.

Inner-Forming˝ encompasses the numerous aspects of your life and your mind. It's where change has to begin in order to take hold effectively and permanently in your life. Because all change starts in the mind, Inner-Forming™ is the mental labor you pursue to direct change in the direction you want it to go.

In your process of setting and achieving goals, Inner-Forming™ is the time and effort you put toward influencing your subconscious mind, building your mental creation of your goals, and installing your chosen beliefs, vision, and self-image in your own mind. Basically, it's programming your own mind to help you achieve what you want.

Outer-Performing™ (which we'll discuss in the next chapter) is the time and effort you put toward building the physical creation of your goals, such as physically working, performing daily tasks, solving real-world problems, interacting with others, and utilizing your time wisely. If your goal is to be physically fit and healthy, a part of your Inner-Forming™ would be spending time visualizing yourself being fit, healthy, and active (and happy about it!), and your Outer-Performing™ would be actually going to the gym, hiking, jogging, or playing sports.

Inner-Forming™ is by far the more powerful of the two, but, of course, both are necessary. In fact, your Inner-Forming™ steers your Outer-Performing™, as well as your end results. It's really your subconscious mind that controls your behavior and results, and your Inner-Forming™ programs or forms your subconscious mind. This is how you have total control over yourself. The whole idea of this book is to help you realize this truth!

Once your vision of your future and improved self-image exist firmly in your subconscious mind as a result of your Inner-Forming™, your circumstances in the physical world will transform into your vision, and you will transform into your new self. This *will* happen. It is inevitable, as sure as day will follow night.

Beginning drivers go through extensive training to learn the nuances of an automobile before they are truly competent to drive. We should expend that kind of energy (or more) to master the powerful machine we call the human mind. It's true that it's possible to learn from experience if you're extremely observant— but think how much more efficient and effective it would be to prepare yourself ahead of time so that your energies would be focused on the most productive activities.

The human mind has an infinite number of powers available to it, to the point that if we tried to develop all of them at one time, the task would be overwhelming. It's far better and more useful to concentrate on a few of the mental arts that have proven to be the most useful in creating a successful life. Here we will focus on four mental arts:

- Visualization

- Positive self-image

- Intuition

- Intention

Visualization

Visualization is the art of creating something out of nothing. If we agree with Stephen Covey that everything is created twice (first in the mind, and then in the actual world), then visualization is the step from which an idea springs into reality. Nothing that has ever been built or achieved in the physical world would exist without the spark of inspiration that appeared first in the mind.

It follows, then, that visualization creates reality out of any human endeavor. Our reality is based on our *perception*, or the way that we see things, filtered through our beliefs and our thoughts. What visualization does is create a mental reality—Covey's first type of creation—based on those thoughts and beliefs.

For example, your life experiences may have led you to the belief that you are capable of building things out of wood. Perhaps you have a patio or a deck in your backyard, and you have thought how nice it would be to have something comfortable to sit on while you enjoy the outdoors. So you get the idea to build some wooden outdoor furniture.

At this point you are at the first stage of visualization. You have a concept—wooden outdoor furniture—that needs refining. When you narrow that concept to a chair, you can begin to visualize specific types of chairs. Then you do research and realize that you want to build an Adirondack chair.

The refinement of your initial concept is one of the key components of effective visualization. Although we learned in school that a noun is a person, place, or thing, there are also abstract nouns, concepts that exist without existing physically. Words such as government, mathematics, and sports are abstract nouns. They cannot be pictured without being narrowed down to more specific images that represent those concepts.

The human mind is powerful, but by definition it is impossible to visualize an abstraction. You have to have a concrete picture in your mind to be able to create it. In our example, we narrowed our idea from furniture to chair to Adirondack chair. Based on your original belief that you are capable of building something out of wood and your decision that an Adirondack chair would fulfill your needs, you can proceed to build an Adirondack chair (which you happily enjoy on your patio, sipping tea while watching the sun set in the evening).

This example is very specific because when it comes to visualizing, specificity is vital. The more specific and concrete the vision of what you want to create, the more power it has on your subconscious mind. It's not enough to say that you want to be rich—you have to envision yourself with the trappings of wealth, in whatever way has the most important associations for you. It might be living in a large home, driving a specific type of car, or even looking at a bank statement that shows a large balance in your account. Find what has the most power for you.

Visualization is a skill that can be developed. In fact, it must be developed if you want to achieve the goals that are most meaningful to you. Most people actually have negative visualizations because they have not trained themselves. When starting something new or challenging, they visualize themselves failing, or they recall images of when they were unsuccessful in the past because remembered images are typically the most vivid. This creates a negative energy that inhibits the chances of success.

The Inner-Forming˜ that you want to do is visualizing something that does not yet exist or has not existed in the past. However, the only reason to repeat something from the past is if you previously achieved the result that you wanted to achieve. Since personal growth stems from achieving new, more ambitious goals, visualizing new objectives is the skill that you must develop.

What you are doing with visualization is basically directed daydreaming. Daydreaming has negative connotations for most of us. We may have been scolded in school for daydreaming or ridiculed by friends for "having our head in the clouds." If your daydreams are simply a way to kill time, then some criticism is due. It's wasteful to use such a powerful tool with no purpose in mind. It's far better to use that ability to make your daydreams actually come true. When you can take your most cherished desires and turn them into images that connect to your subconscious, you are constructing a new life for yourself, one of achievement and success.

Maximizing Visualization's Power

One of the main principles to maximize the power of visualization is to *take it seriously*. Our lives reflect what we focus on the most. If you fritter away time daydreaming or spend your energy visualizing trivialities, then you are squandering an opportunity. Visualization is a powerful tool that has been proven effective, and you must take it seriously if you want to make changes in your life.

Professional and Olympic athletes regularly use visualization to help them compete better. Research has consistently shown that performance actually improves after visualization. One such study on Russian Olympic athletes used a control group with no visualization in addition to their training, then three other groups with varying degrees of visualization and lesser amounts of training. The group with the most improvement was the one that actually did the least physical training but the most visualization.

Golfers use visualization to improve their swings, and basketball players use it to improve their shooting. All manner of competitors who are devoted to improving their performance believe in visualization as an essential part of their training.

You can also maximize your visualization skills by practicing them when you are calm, relaxed, and focused. The human mind has been compared to a barking dog, paying attention to whatever comes its way. With all the distractions that assault us in today's society, it's even more important that you find time to spend in a meditative state of mind.

When you are physically relaxed, your subconscious mind becomes more receptive to the images that you introduce to it. Find a quiet place where you will be undisturbed for a few minutes. A room with dim lighting and a comfortable chair is beneficial. Become aware of the tightness of your muscles and consciously relax them. Let your shoulders drop, and breathe evenly and deeply.

While this is not meditation, it is similar in many ways because you are making it possible for your mind to calm itself. As the distractions of the outer world begin to fade, bring the image of your goal into focus. Remember, the more concrete your image, the greater impact it has on your subconscious mind.

As you envision your goal, pay attention to your feelings and emotions. The proper goal should bring you happiness. At this point, you are neither wondering how you're going to achieve or create your goal, nor are you remembering past failures. You are simply creating an image of something that gives you joy, something that does not yet exist.

What you are doing with this process is similar to the Chinese philosophy of *yin* and *yang*. Yin and yang represent the opposites that are a part of life. In the process of visualization, you are both relaxed and focused. You are directing your imagination, yet you are doing it as effortlessly as possible. You should not have to strain to see your vision.

This is a skill that has to be developed through practice. It can take time for most people to picture a concrete image. Other images may try to intrude. In our example above, different types of chairs or furniture might compete for your attention. Calmly let the other images slip away until you have the one you want, the one that brings you pleasure.

What Do I Visualize?

In the example above, the chair was a simple image, reflecting a simple goal. With other goals, your visualizations may be more complex, in which case you want to spend some time beforehand answering questions. There are a number of questions you might ask yourself:

What kind of person will I be? Our programming often misleads us when it comes to what type of people are successful. For example, if you have been programmed to believe that money is the root of all evil, it's difficult to imagine that you can both achieve wealth and be a caring, loving person. The truth, of course, is that you choose what kind of person you will be, regardless of your level of success.

Rather than being selfish, your image can reflect the kindness and patience you will have in your new reality. A successful life is not only about material wealth, but also about the growth you can achieve as a human being. In your vision, you can reflect all the positive attributes that define the concept of humanity.

How will I behave? Our actions reflect what kind of person we are. In the example above, you might visualize yourself as a loving, caring person of wealth in a position to help those who are less fortunate by creating endowments or bestowing scholarships.

You can envision yourself as a mentor, advising those who are struggling to work their way up in the world. There are key times in the lives of most people when a helping hand can make a huge difference. When you create the vision of yourself as a successful person, you have the opportunity to be the kind of person who makes a difference in the lives of those around him or her.

Visualization is a way of not only *predicting* the future, but *creating* it—creating a future that does not yet exist.

The Self-Image

Here is a saying that I sincerely believe: you never outperform your self-image. Your image of yourself, and the sense of identity that stems from it, affects everything you think or do. Whether you think you can or can't do something is a reflection of your self-image. This single factor determines—and sometimes restricts—the options that you see as available to you, regardless of the number of actual opportunities that may exist.

Your self-image is what has been created from all the programming that has gone on in your life. It is your perception of your abilities, appearance, reputation, and all the other facets of your personality.

In recent years large numbers of articles, news stories, and studies have been devoted to the subject of appearance, self-image, and their effect on young women. The standard put forth in the media (in advertising, television, and movies) has been that of a thin female, thin almost to the point of emaciation. Furthermore, female celebrities who gain weight are often ridiculed in gossip tabloids and columns.

As a result of this standard, many young women and girls who are at a healthy weight and body composition view themselves as too fat. Their self-images have been affected by the programming that occurs from the impact of the media's message. That self-image in many cases is incorrect, and is simply based on what modern society and celebrity culture have told them.

If you view yourself as unattractive, awkward, clumsy, or in some other negative manner, then your options will be limited. That is, your limitations will be imposed because of your view of yourself, not because any of the descriptions are true. If you think of yourself in a certain way, you will only consider those options that coincide with your opinion. If you think of yourself as clumsy, then you will reject the idea of becoming an athlete. If you think of yourself as unattractive, then you will shun social occasions. If you think of yourself as a loser, then you will reject any opportunity to help you win. Your behavior conforms to your self-image.

If you want to analyze your own self-image, look at the results that you have achieved thus far in your life. Your current life situation is a direct result of your self-image. Your hobbies, social life, occupation, and everything else are reflections of how you view yourself and what type of person you think you are.

When you look at the results you have achieved in your life, are you satisfied? If not, the good news is that you can make changing your self-image a part of your Inner-Forming". It stands to reason that if your past results are a product of your self-image, then future results can be improved with an improved self-image.

Using visualization, picture yourself in the future. You have realized all of your dreams and achieved all your goals. You are a happy person living a fulfilled life full of love and joy that you share with others. Are you able to create that vision of yourself?

Many times, a person's self-image is so distorted that they can't envision themselves ever being successful and happy. If you find this vision difficult, then make a game out of it. Ask yourself, "What if I were to achieve all my goals? What if I were successful and happy?" You're not trying to force your mind to accept the concept as a hard reality—you're simply creating the *possibility* of it. When it comes to adjusting your self-image, it's this possibility that is important. When you acknowledge that a happy, successful life is possible, then your subconscious mind adjusts your self-image accordingly. Your options are no longer restricted by your negative self-image, and you are now someone who has potential.

Suddenly, you will be presented with a wide-open future. Your self-image, which controls all of your actions, options, and opportunities, will broaden to accept the idea that you can obtain improved results that are better than what you have had in the past.

As a result of this new vision, you will experience wonder and excitement at the possibilities that the future holds for you. Your subconscious mind associates these pleasurable feelings with your new self-image, reinforcing it. What you have done is created a cycle of looking ahead with optimism.

When you have hope, it energizes you, giving you confidence and strength. Achieving your goals still requires planning, work, and effort, of course—that's part of your Outer-Performing". But changing your self-image so that you are able to access the resources already available to you is a major part of your Inner-Forming".

Intuition

As wonderful as the human mind is, we as humans are not able to precisely calculate all the ramifications of our actions. The world is too complex for such calculation. That's why we have been blessed with *intuition.*

What is intuition (also called the *intuitive factor*)? It's our ability to discern information from a situation, even when we can't quite put our finger on what that information is. We often call it a vibe, a hunch, a feeling, or an impression. Intuition is our subconscious mind telling us something without going through the conscious mind, which relies on language. Remember, the whole purpose of Inner-Forming" is to mold our subconscious mind into a powerful partner who helps us achieve our goals. So when our super-powerful partner communicates back to us, we should listen. The more we develop our intuition, the quicker we will succeed.

Because the subconscious mind is so perceptive, it's important that we pay attention to our emotions—our "gut feeling"—when it comes to appraising situations. Often our decisions cannot be based on the tangible information that is available. Either there is not enough information, the information that is available may indicate conflicting conclusions, or the information may be so complex that a so-called "logical" decision cannot be made. In these types of situation, the most reliable decisions are often made through intuition.

To receive the most benefit from your intuition, a couple of factors have to be in place. For one thing, you have to be *in the moment.* You must be completely focused on the situation, idea, or option that is presented to you. This skill is more difficult than it sounds because as a society we are accustomed to being distracted. Once again, however, it is a skill that can be developed with practice.

The other factor that is required is that you need to be completely aware of your feelings and emotions. This factor is more common. Have you ever been presented with something that feels too good to be true? While good fortune happens to all of us at various times in our lives, when our subconscious mind communicates with us via our emotions, it's wise to pay attention. There are often signals that the subconscious picks up that our other senses don't detect.

Use your intuition and develop it. A plan often cannot be calculated thoroughly up to its conclusion. You simply have to rely on what feels right and take action. If you insist on only pursuing those courses of action that lead to a fully foreseeable conclusion, then you will miss out on many opportunities that can make the difference between achieving your goals and failing.

One word of caution must be mentioned here. If necessary, compare the direction your intuition leads you in with your most fundamental values before you take action. By definition, using your intuition is not an exact science. After all, it works through your subconscious mind, which can sometimes seem fickle.

Using your value system to examine your intuitive decisions can help you separate false messages from true ones. It may feel good to seize an opportunity that immediately presents itself, but not at the expense of violating your integrity or honesty. Self-indulgent whims are not the same as intuition. With practice, using and trusting your intuition will make intuitive decisions more accurate and reliable.

Remember that your intuition can guide you at times when mere facts are either insufficient or overwhelming. If you remain in the moment and stay attentive to your feelings, you will reap the benefits of using your intuition.

Importance of Intention

In the television series *Star Trek*, the captain often gave his crew the orders to "set a course." That told them where, in the vastness of space, they should direct the ship. You must set a course every day so that you can direct the benefits of your Inner-Forming¨ to the direction you want. When you properly set this direction and then begin to take action, the feeling of your intention will remain a subtle, underlying force, enhancing your subsequent actions. This feeling will assist you in achieving your intentions. It is through *intention* that you begin to translate your Inner-Forming¨ to outer results. It brings meaning and purpose to your actions and to your life.

The first thing every morning, before you get busy with your day, decide in what direction you want your day to go. Approach each day with intent, with purpose. Know what you want to get accomplished so that you can focus your natural gifts and efforts to that end. Do the same before taking any important action or making any important decisions. Bring all your powers to focus on doing the best you can.

Before I enter a meeting, I always try to spend a few minutes of quiet time setting my intention for the meeting and visualizing the meeting going well. In my experience this creates an energy about me that accompanies me into the meeting and helps me be effective. People can feel it!

Natural Process

Each of us has been blessed with innate gifts that nature has given us. Spending time doing your Inner-Forming" in the areas I've described is a way to coordinate your energies with nature. The gifts of intuition, visualization, intention, and the ability to craft your own self-image can be developed as part of a natural process that maximizes your success.

Process, as defined by the dictionary, is "a systematic series of actions directed to some end." You can methodically work with your inner gifts to develop them fully. Recognizing Inner-Forming" as a natural process, you can't force its progress, nor can you deny its development when it happens. You must *cooperate* with nature.

First of all, be open to learning about yourself. The ancient Greek dictum *know thyself* must be part of your philosophy for growth. This doesn't mean becoming overly critical of yourself. It means being aware that as a human being you have strengths as well as weaknesses, and must accommodate them accordingly. Awareness of your own qualities is the first step.

You must also resist the temptations of negative outside influences. As you develop your own programming, designed to maximize your chances for success, you will often run into others who have their own ideas of how you should be programmed. With modern society as chaotic and frenetic as it is, it's safe to say that societal programming usually runs counter to those of a self-aware, growing individual.

There is nothing mysterious about doing Inner-Forming™ as part of a natural process, other than the fact that most people are not willing to do it. You can practically guarantee your own success by working on these areas. Trying to bypass Inner-Forming™ can at best result in only temporary semi-victories.

Other effective techniques of Inner-Forming™ are:

- Reading your goal statement twice each day with feeling

- Repeating positive affirmations

- Practicing meditation

- Managing your inner speech

All your Inner-Forming™ techniques combine to create changes within yourself, your beliefs, and your thoughts, and then these changes must be expressed through your daily physical actions— your Outer-Performing™. You'll waste a lot of time if you don't learn to do your Outer-Performing™ effectively, so let's learn how to maximize your efforts.

8

Outer-Performing™

By thought, the thing you want is brought to you;
by action you receive it.

—Wallace D. Wattles

Your daily physical actions (your Outer-Performing") will be unique to you and your situation. However, in this chapter we'll discuss these powerful principles of how to manage and supercharge your daily actions so you can accelerate your success big-time:

- Important vs. Unimportant Activities

- Your Daily Agenda

- Time Management

- Continued Learning

- Finding Creative Solutions

- Calculated Risks

Keep in mind that your Outer-Performing™ is the manifestation and continuation of your Inner-Forming™. Together they form a complete package, where purposeful self-creation results in powerful successful action.

Important Activities

The first key principle is the idea of distinguishing between important activities and unimportant activities. What I mean by important activities is the activities that have the greatest positive impact on your success. The simple act of going through and classifying each of your daily activities as important or unimportant can be a real eye-opener. High achievers spend the majority of their time engaging in important activities, and it makes sense to emulate what successful people do.

What's so important about important activities? Look at it this way: maybe you want to go on a trip. You've decided where you want to go, you've made hotel reservations so you'll have a place to sleep, and you've made arrangements at work so you can take time off. The time comes to leave, and you go outside and get in your car. You wait expectantly to arrive at your destination.

You'll wait a long time because you've failed to engage in the important activity of starting your car and actually driving to your destination! In the same way, many people do all the preparations to achieve success but don't actually engage in the action that will take them there. Sitting in one place and then expecting your destination to come to you doesn't work.

The word *activity* is based on the word *act*. According to the dictionary, *to act* means "to do something, to exert energy or force." If you exert energy or force, then something's going to move. In your journey to achieve success, the object that moves is *you*. Whether you define success as going on vacation or becoming a millionaire, you have to move in order to change your life in the proper way.

When you use your time to engage in important activities, you are moving toward your goal of success, however you define it. Some of the activities may be minor, such as getting out of bed when your alarm goes off rather than hitting the snooze button. Other activities may be large, such as enrolling in a class or attending a seminar. Important activities may be large or small, but they always produce results.

For most people, their job or business contains two or three specific actions that produce almost all the results. If you identify those specific actions, you can direct most of your effort to doing them well and your results will increase significantly.

Whether you watch her television show or not, Martha Stewart is a great example of focusing on important activities. She presents herself as expert at all kinds of skills, from cooking to home decorating to entertaining guests at a dinner party to making her own decorations. The amazing thing is that she really *is* good at all of those activities.

During an interview, Martha Stewart was once asked if there was anything that she *wasn't* good at. After a moment's thought, Stewart replied, "I'm not good at games, at wasting time. I'm always doing something. If I get bored with cooking, I go work in the garden. If I get bored with that, I work on crafts to decorate the home. I'm always working on something." Her devotion to staying busy has helped her achieve enormous success.

Besides moving you toward success, when you engage in important activities, you add density and texture to your life. Everyone has had a day at work or a weekend day when they've "vegged out" in front of the television or the computer screen. After a while, they look up and realize that they've squandered hours doing something that adds zero value to their life.

On the other hand, everyone has had a time when they stayed busy and productive, and at the end of the day, looked back with satisfaction on what they accomplished.

You add density to your world when you create something through your actions that is more than just a momentary distraction. Civilization is built upon the work of artists, writers, architects, and other builders that create things that last. In your own way, you do the same when you do what you consider important work. At the same time, you add texture to yourself by becoming a more interesting person—face it, people who *do things* are much more interesting than those who don't.

Your important activities are the activities that you've chosen to help you achieve your dreams. They will differ from the activities of other people because others will have their own dreams. Large or small, it's the actions you take that will help you fulfill your dreams and realize your full potential.

How, then, do you determine what actions are important? They are the activities that produce positive results and move you closer to your goals.

Going back to the example I gave earlier, getting up immediately when your alarm clock goes off gives you extra time compared to lying in bed. It's the first step in your day. How you make use of that time is the next important activity. If you plop down in front of the television and watch cartoons for two hours, then you've squandered the opportunity that you gave yourself.

On the other hand, if you use the extra time to study, to work out, or to make plans for your day, then you have started your day working toward your success. You are working at producing positive results. Getting up with the alarm is your first important activity, which sets in motion other activities that will help you achieve success.

If important activities are the ones that produce positive results, then it's important that you know what results you want. You establish these desired results through your goal-setting and your Inner-Forming˜. For example, if one of your goals is to develop a healthy, physically fit body, then working out in the morning is a proven way to achieve that result. You've studied and done research that confirm exercise is the best way to achieve your goal. Therefore, exercise produces a positive result for you.

When you commit to spending your time on important activities, you recognize that you are living a success-oriented life. Your actions are oriented and directed toward success. Because of that direction, you are no longer sitting on the sidelines, but you are instead in the game.

Some people confuse activity with action and busyness with achievement. They believe that energy is all that matters. Of course, taking action requires energy, but mindless activity for its own sake is just as self-defeating as doing nothing. Your actions should be thought-out and geared toward moving you closer to your goals.

If you are more used to wasting time than using your time, the thought of investing your time on important activities may seem somewhat intimidating. The good news is that when you develop the habit of working on those things that are most important to you, you are reinforcing your success mentality. It will eventually become easier to do the things you should be doing. When you take time to examine how you're spending your time—something you should do periodically—you will find that you have wisely invested that time.

Unimportant Activities

Once you understand the definition of *important* activities, it becomes somewhat easier to identify *unimportant* activities. Whereas important activities take you closer to your goals, unimportant activities keep you in place or even move you further away from what you want to achieve. They are the activities that have little or no impact on achieving success.

If most people were to do an analysis of how they spend their time, they would find that most of their day is spent involved in nonproductive, unimportant activities. For example, watching television is probably the biggest time waster in our lives. According to a 2008 report by the A. C. Nielsen Company, which measures television viewing habits, the average American watches more than 127 hours of television a month. Sure, there are educational programs available, but the millions of viewers are not putting those shows at the top of the ratings. We are squandering our days and nights watching throwaway television.

Think of what you could do with an extra 127 hours a month. Learning a language, developing new skills, exercising more—you could accomplish almost anything if you devoted that much time to it. Unfortunately, most of us don't do what we know we should do. Most people take the easy way out by plopping into a comfortable chair and spending the entire evening watching television. Even during those times when we're not watching television, we focus primarily on activities that distract us for a while.

Each of us, high achievers and low performers alike, have a finite amount of time during a day. What's more, we each have the exact same amount of time during a day—24 hours. The difference between the high achiever and the low performer is how each decides to spend his or her time.

This information is not particularly earth-shaking, and it's certainly not new. Making the most of your time has been espoused by leaders and philosophers for thousands of years. Yet, most people waste most of their days and end up with a life full of regrets. Why don't we do more with our time?

For many people, it's simply a lack of awareness. These are the people who have never been exposed to the concepts of achieving success or who have heard of the concepts but don't grasp them. These unfortunate people simply stroll through their days. They have no direction or purpose other than solving the problem that's directly in front of them without any thought of future consequences. This type of person is often caught by surprise or has a lot of emergencies that could have been prevented with a little forethought.

There are also those who want to succeed, but lack training. They are eager and energetic, but their energy is unfocused because they don't have a thorough understanding of the principles of success or the tools they need to succeed. They waste time and energy on nonproductive activities in the hope that they will achieve success through brute force.

Unfortunately, most people engage in unimportant activities because they simply lack drive. These are the people who have accepted their programming and who have become comfortable in their misery. They have been beaten down by life and by their own minds to the extent that the idea of actually exerting energy to achieve a goal is more than they can take. They shrug off suggestions that there might be more to life than what they perceive. It usually takes a traumatic event to shake these people out of their complacency.

There are also those few souls who have worked hard to embrace the successful mind-set and lifestyle but fall out of the habit of using their time wisely. Something may have happened that threw them out of their routine, and their old habits reasserted themselves. In any case, such backsliding can happen to anyone. These folks simply need to have their attention refocused. Getting in the habit of assessing your progress toward your goals is a good way to determine if you have fallen out of the success mind-set.

Your Inner-Forming" will mold your success habits into what you need to reach your goals, and it does it in a quiet, subtle, and unfailing way.

Your Daily Agenda

If you want to begin using your time more wisely, then you are in luck. More time-management tools are available today than ever before. Planners, organizers, alarms, appointment books, prioritizers—you can become overwhelmed with all the choices. So it's important that you begin with the basics.

The way to start working on your time management is through your daily agenda. A daily agenda is a written record that helps you organize your day. Whether you use an expensive organizer or a cheap tablet, it's important that you find some way to determine how you will spend your day.

I emphasize using a daily agenda because most of us work in the units of a business day. When planning your activities, using a daily format makes the process easier to grasp and to control. By using a daily agenda, you can work out ways to anticipate the future and to record the past. It's a method for learning that can't be beat.

The daily agenda is also important because it can help you minimize the time you spend on unimportant activities. Although no one is able to do away with all of the distractions and time wasters that occur beyond our control, purposeful planning of your day can reduce their impact. The goal is to engage in as many important activities as possible during your day.

The main benefit of the daily agenda, however, is that it provides a way for you to keep score. You can track your actions and observe exactly what results they produced. Keeping score is important because it provides you with an indicator of your progress toward your goals. You have to actually see forward movement to be able to honestly say that you are making progress.

Without some type of record, the danger is that you will begin swimming in circles. Your record of how you spend your time ensures that your progress is forward, not simply standing still. Remember, energy is necessary for success, but energy alone does not ensure success.

How do you keep score? First of all, you have to know what the final result you want looks like. This is where your vision of the future becomes so important. Realizing that vision is your goal. To reach that goal, you establish objectives that take you to that goal. In other words, you create a process that, when complete, achieves what you want to achieve. The steps in that process are the activities in which you should engage.

It's important that you break your objectives down into observable steps. It should be clear when you have accomplished a particular step in the process. At that point, the activity that helped you finish that step may no longer be necessary. In such a case, an important activity has become an unimportant activity. Your daily agenda will help you make sure that every day is spent on activities that will help you achieve the next level in your progress.

Time Management

What I'm talking about, of course, is *time management*. The term "time management" is a bit deceptive, because you can't really manage time. Time is a finite resource that is distributed steadily—60 seconds to a minute, 60 minutes to an hour, 24 hours to a day. You cannot increase the number of hours you have in a day.

When we say time management, we are actually referring to *self-management*. We can't control time, but we can manage how we use the time we have. Deliberate planning is the key to effective time management. Effective time management is vital to anyone who wants to achieve ongoing success. Trimming away unnecessary activities is the only way to continually improve yourself.

By monitoring the results of your time management plan, you can see where you need to focus your attention. For example, you may feel more productive or energetic at certain times of the day. Use those times for activities that require more mental or physical energy. Try to schedule low-impact activities such as checking email for times when your energy level may be a bit lower.

With the number of time management tools available to you, find a format that works for you. Some people enjoy using computer software and multiple alarms and reminders from various electronic devices. What works for one person may not work for another, so it can take time for you to become comfortable with a system. The main thing to keep in mind is that whatever you use, it is only a tool. If it doesn't work for you, don't be afraid to adapt it or even discard it for another method that is more effective.

Continued Learning

The most vital Outer-Performing¨ that you can do is to continue learning. Continued learning is important for several reasons. For one thing, the world is always changing. Skills that are highly valued become less so as technology develops. The marketplace changes. For many college graduates, much of what they learn in school is obsolete within just a few years. In a world of constant change, adaptability is key, and the best way to become adaptable is to learn something new.

Besides increasing your adaptability, continued learning can help you improve your plans. Plans, like people, need to be flexible and adaptable. It's foolish to continue with a plan exactly as it is when new information becomes available that affects the situation. Detours are a regular part of any trip, and it's a foolhardy traveler that tries to push through road construction instead of going around.

Another reason to continue learning is because you may have made errors in your original plan. Despite our best efforts, human beings are prone to mistakes. Becoming mistake-free is an admirable goal, but not a very realistic one. The best you can do is to try to recognize mistakes as soon as they happen and to correct your errors.

These errors might not have been apparent at your previous level of awareness and education. It's only with new information and knowledge that you realize you made the error. Without your commitment to continued learning, such errors remain in place and uncorrected. Those errors are the ones that can throw your entire plan awry.

Finding Creative Solutions

When it comes to your planning skills, you may have heard the phrase "think outside the box." What does that mean, and why is it important? *Thinking outside the box* means looking at a situation from a different perspective. Established patterns of thinking can become a hindrance simply because they don't take into consideration other options.

When you look at a situation creatively, you are often able to come up with solutions to problems that would otherwise be ignored. Swiss engineer George de Mestral came up with the idea for Velcro fasteners after going hiking with his dog. When he returned home, he found that his dog and his boots were covered with burrs. Curious, he examined them under a microscope. He used the principles that made the burrs stick to material to invent a fabric that could be fastened and unfastened, the fabric we know as Velcro.

Such ideas have a sort of elegance to them. They are elegant in the sense that they have a simple solution to resolve a particular problem or situation. Often it's only by looking around at established ideas that you are able to find the most elegant solution.

When you want to develop your creative thinking, try to come up with ideas that are similar in some way, even if they are in a completely different areas. Architects often design their buildings with the idea of replicating a structure that occurs in nature. A flower or a plant has a structure, and so does a building. By looking for similarities in these otherwise dissimilar objects, architects have managed to create beautiful and functional buildings.

An analogy to this is the game of chess. Because of the number of pieces and the variety of moves they can make, the total number of possible moves in a given position is astronomical, well beyond the capacity of a human being to calculate. What chess masters do, however, is look for patterns, ways in which a given position is similar to other situations that they have seen before. The two positions may be different, but they are the same in key ways, so that the plan for one works with the other.

To develop this outside-the-box-planning, try to always keep an open mind. It's okay to have opinions, of course, but when looking for a solution, be receptive to any idea that may show merit. Even a bad idea may have key parts that are workable.

Also, make sure that you respond based on good information. You want to have the facts straight before embarking on a solution. Being sure of your facts will help you look for ideas in other ways because you will know what factors are important.

When confronted with a situation that calls for ideas, ask yourself "What does this remind me of?" Use your imagination and don't be afraid to look silly. Seeing similarities between different situations is a very powerful tool for anyone who craves the best answers.

Calculated Risks

Finally, your Outer-Performing˵ requires that you occasionally take calculated risks. A *risk* is any action for which you don't know the outcome. Your willingness to take calculated risks is your recognition that everything in life is not knowable. If you always wait to take action until you can be 100 percent positive of the result, then a large part of the time you will be frozen in place.

Please note that I'm not talking about taking foolish risks. Recklessness eventually leads to failure. Risks that have been considered, planned, and allowed for, on the other hand, will often pay dividends. A calculated risk is one that has been measured and weighed. Meaning, the consequences for its failure are weighed.

Calculations to maximize the chances of success have been used so that, as much as possible, you have stacked the odds in your favor.

Ultimately, however, taking a risk boils down to judgment. When you consider the possible benefits versus the possible costs, you have to decide, based on relevant experience and knowledge, as to whether the risk is worth it or not.

Consider the entrepreneur who wants to open his own business. There is no way for him to be certain that the business will be profitable. He conducts market research, looks at the competition, and finds any other pertinent information he can so that when he opens his business it will be a well-thought-out, *calculated* risk.

President Theodore Roosevelt once said

> *The credit belongs to the man who is actually in the arena,*
> *whose face is marred by dust and sweat and blood; who strives*
> *valiantly; who errs, who comes short again and again, because*
> *there is no effort without error and shortcoming; but who does*
> *actually strive to do the deeds; who knows great enthusiasms,*
> *the great devotions; who spends himself in a worthy cause; who*
> *at the best knows in the end the triumph of high achievement,*
> *and who at the worst, if he fails, at least fails while daring*
> *greatly; so that his place shall never be with those cold and*
> *timid souls who neither know victory nor defeat.*

Outer-Performing™ is all about physically doing, and you can apply the principles in this chapter to energize and maximize your time and effort in physically doing activities. When a seed remains dormant, it is only a seed. It's only after it takes the action of pushing through the soil and stretching toward the sun that it realizes its full potential and becomes a plant.

As you begin to "push through the soil" by taking effective action toward your goals, you will undoubtedly have to interact with other human beings. Probably a lot of human beings. In utilizing the help of others to help you achieve your goals, you'll benefit immensely by developing a strong ability to communicate effectively with other people. That's the subject of the next chapter.

9
Creating Teammates

Everything in the world we want to do or get done,
we must do with and through people.

—Earl Nightingale

It's said that in the forecourt of the Temple of Apollo at Delphi, there was an inscription written in Greek that said "Know thyself." (For those of us who are less classically inclined, the same phrase—in Latin—was written above the Oracle's door in *The Matrix*.) To be successful, it's important to know yourself. But to ensure success, you have to be able to control your mind and your actions so that you are a leader to yourself as well as to other people.

To lead a complete and successful life, you first have to learn how to lead yourself, and then you have to learn to be a leader of others. Knowing your own mind is the main obstacle to most people, but it is the one trait that leads to true success. Once you're on the way to mastering yourself, you become a beacon to other people—we are attracted to those who have self assurance about what they want in life.

As the philosopher John Donne once said, "No man is an island." No matter what type of success anyone has, at least part of it is due to the efforts of other people. Lance Armstrong won the Tour de France, cycling's greatest race, seven times. Sitting on a bicycle and riding hundreds of miles would seem to be one of the most solitary endeavors you could think of. Armstrong, however, could not have won the Tour de France without the help of his teammates and the rest of his support crew.

In the same way, you need to make sure that you have your own support crew to help you achieve your goals. What is the best way to get what you want? *Help others get what* they *want.* There's no mystery about this fact. Whether you call it the giant wheel of karma or the universal law of reciprocity, the belief is that whatever you do in life eventually returns to you. Helping other people is the surest way to be able to count on their help when you need it.

Each of us interacts with other people. Most of these interactions are very casual, with little emotional involvement, but they still leave an impression on the people we encounter. All these interactions build your reputation with others—people form a picture of you based on how you speak to them, how you follow through on your promises, and any one of the thousands of other points of contact you have with them.

When you develop a reputation for helping others, you increase your integrity level with not only the person you helped, but with the people they tell. If you have a reputation for integrity, people are more likely to help you. Simply by doing what most people consider the right thing to do, you are nurturing relationships that can prove helpful to you.

What I am *not* saying here is that you should interact with other people in a manipulative way. To help others for selfish motives undermines the whole point of this belief. It's not the fact of your helping that is important, but that you help others unselfishly, without thought of getting a return on your "investment." Paradoxically, it's by helping others without thought of reward that you eventually get the most reward.

If we equate the quality of your life with the quality of the questions you ask, then the question "How can I help?" should be close to the top of the list. In any situation, others will always appreciate a genuine offer of help. When you make that offer, you automatically improve the quality of your own life. You are aspiring to have higher morals, to gain a higher set of values than one of mere self-interest.

In all of your forms of communication, you are projecting a particular type of image. Your actions are more important than your choice of words and your actions tell others more about you, but you still have to keep your communication in mind. Whether it's personal contact, written messages, or speaking to someone on the phone, you will project an image of helpfulness if that is your sincere concern. Mahatma Gandhi spoke to millions of people through public speeches and one-on-one conversations, but his deeds left a greater legacy than any of his speeches. As he once said, "You must be the change that you want to see in the world."

How do you go about meeting the needs of others? In some ways it's as simple as making the offer, but in others the process is very complex. One important point is to *know the person*. You will, of course, have the occasional opportunity to help a stranger whose needs are straightforward—helping with a flat tire, for instance. And performing random acts of kindness for strangers is a wonderful habit to develop.

What I mean when I say *know the person* is that you should understand what the person really needs. You can only know this if you care about the person and have empathy for them. Put yourself in the shoes of the other person and see if what they appear to need is all that you can do. You may have acquaintances that obviously need financial help—they may even need food—but to give them money might offend them or injure their pride. It would be better to offer them an opportunity to work, to perform some job for you where they could *earn* the money instead. There is dignity in work, and instead of feeling humiliated by receiving charity, they could feel pride in providing for themselves and their family. This is the type of fact that you could only know if you were familiar with the person involved.

Other times a person may ask for something that is the exact opposite of what they need. An alcoholic might ask you to buy him a drink. Is that what the person really needs? Or would he be better served by buying him a hearty meal? Giving without contemplation is often the wholly wrong thing to do, even if it's done in the right spirit. Helping others is more than giving them cash, patting them on the head, and sending them on their way.

Sometimes you have to look at the bigger picture and what it takes to give virtuously. That is, what it takes to help the other person achieve higher levels of existence for himself or herself. When helping others, take into consideration the idea that you want to help them meet their *needs*.

Having such an outlook toward helping others is not an exact science. Giving and helping with the right spirit is vital in those cases where what a person needs is not clear. Often, of course, you simply have to help them in the way they requested. Nonetheless, you want to give with full awareness to what kind of help you are providing, and not simply go through the motions, doing what's easiest for you. To help others in the right way, with the proper reverence for their dignity and humanity, is how you can aspire to the highest level of spirituality for yourself.

Communication

As you might imagine, being able to communicate well is key to interacting with other people. Television sitcoms use miscommunication as a standard plot device for their 22 minute shows. Clear communication would often resolve a problem within minutes, but then there would be no show.

Fortunately for all of us, real life is not a television show. We have the ability to avoid and solve problems simply by communicating well. Excellence in communication is something that you can develop if you care enough and take the time to learn it. If you convey your message to others effectively, that will become part of your reputation as well.

The message you emit to others is of prime importance. It's one of the key components of your relationships. Miscommunication (or *no* communication) can unnecessarily derail a relationship, especially with those close to you. If you communicate poorly, the other party can get the wrong message or something completely different from what you intended.

Although you may not realize it, you communicate with other people hundreds or thousands of times a day. Every word, every sound, every look, and every gesture sends a message. Sometimes the other person gets the message subliminally, without realizing that they have received communication from you. Babies read facial expressions constantly, looking for signs of how they should react. With adults, the message may be more subtle, but the communication is still there. Training can help you coordinate all the signals you send so that your message is clear on all levels.

What I'm talking about here is *purposeful* communication. Purposeful communication is sending the precise message that you want the other person to receive. When you do that, you communicate in a way so that everyone stays focused on the purpose you intended, instead of going on incorrect tangents. Try to always communicate with a purpose.

Of course, that doesn't mean that you always have to speak in 100 percent correct, businesslike prose. When you visit with friends, your purpose might be to build camaraderie and good fellowship. Your language will be casual and good-natured. When you speak to a family member, you may be trying to strengthen your relationship, and your language could be gentle, with a warm tone. In any case, your communication has a *purpose*.

You also need to know the situation in which you're communicating, and adapt *how* you communicate accordingly. For example, if you're a manager and a member of your team suddenly begins performing poorly, your first impulse might be to reprimand him for slacking off. As a good communicator, however, you should try to discover exactly what the cause of the drop-off is. Through investigation you find that the team member had a death in the family that has caused him emotional turmoil. Suddenly the situation has changed. Instead of an emotionally-charged "chew out" session, you empathize with him and take the opportunity to offer help and support. Your communication improved because you met the person's need rather than added to his burden.

Many offices suffer from poor morale because the staff is required to attend meetings where a speaker meanders, takes forever to get to the point, or even never really makes a point. Everyone's valuable time is wasted. When you communicate, make sure that your message is clear in your own mind. It saves time and avoids unnecessary problems. Many communication difficulties can be solved merely by making sure of what you want to communicate before you open your mouth.

Are You Really Listening?

A rule of thumb for good communicators to follow is based on advice from the Greek philosopher Epictetus—"We have two ears and one mouth so that we can listen twice as much as we speak." Listening skills are among the most important skills that anyone can have. When we listen to another person, we pay them respect. We recognize the other party has something important to say. Few things in life are as humiliating as speaking to someone who clearly isn't listening and who doesn't really care what we have to say.

By *listening*, I'm not talking about letting the other person speak while you nod politely, saying "uh huh" or "okay" at the appropriate times, waiting for your turn to talk. Listening is an activity. It requires effort and practice to develop the skills necessary to become a good listener. People communicate so much more than just their words when they speak. As a good listener, you need to listen with your ears, your eyes, and your heart.

With your ears, you obviously listen to the words the other speaker is saying. What do the words mean? The dictionary definition of a word is its *denotation*, the technical description of what it means. However, words also carry *connotation*, associated meanings of a word that are defined by the context, expression, and shared experiences of the listener and the speaker. Connotations in a conversation often mean much more than the dictionary meanings of the words, since everyone has some verbal shorthand, jargon, or code words they use.

You also use your ears to listen for the pitch, tone, speed, and volume of what the speaker is saying. These clues can provide the context that accompanies the words themselves. Emotion is much more often expressed these ways, confirming or contradicting what the speaker is saying. Familiarity with the speaker is important in judging these details because different cultures communicate in different ways. Southerners often speak more slowly than people from the north, and people from large families often speak louder than those from smaller families. Don't mistake a cultural trait for an emotion.

Good listeners also use their eyes while listening, to see if gestures and facial expressions match the words. Again, culture plays a significant role in nonverbal communication, so use your past experiences with the person to determine if the physical indicators you observe are inconsistent with the speaker's normal personality. Good poker players often read these physical signs (called "tells") to gather information about their opponents' cards. People often unconsciously reveal their true feelings in their physical actions even when they are trying to hide them.

The most advanced listening skill is to listen with your heart. Listening with your heart means that you listen for the emotion in the speaker's voice and understand the human circumstances that underlie the speaker's words. Understanding another person takes work and caring, both traits of a good listener. When you can emotionally sense where another person's words are coming from, you can ensure that you respond appropriately.

For example, a teenager who takes the time to talk to a parent about trouble he's having in school may be simply complaining, or he may be expressing frustration and indirectly asking for help without wanting to appear as though he's asking for it. As a listener, being aware of the emotional turmoil that many teenagers often experience can make the interaction more rewarding, rather than having it become combative and frustrating for you both. (Replace the word "parent" with "manager" and the word "teenager" with "salesperson," and you have a similar dynamic.)

Listening well improves the accuracy of any communication, and it may be the most important skill you can ever develop.

You discover much more by listening with your eyes and heart in addition to your ears. More importantly, you can adjust your own message or communication technique to suit various situations more effectively. If you realize that learning is a lifelong endeavor, you already know that you have much you can learn from other people. As Ralph Waldo Emerson said, "Every man I meet is in some way my superior; and in that I can learn of him."

Knowing Your Audience

It should be clear by now that in communication, the better you know your audience, the more effectively you can transfer information. This information may be factual or it may be emotional. Your ability to demonstrate leadership to others is based largely on your ability to effectively communicate. To effectively communicate, you should know who you're speaking to and judge the situation. This will help you determine when your communications need to address the factual aspects and when they need to address the emotional aspects of the situation.

Your judgment will be much more accurate when you are aware of the concerns of the other party. For example, a salesperson who talks about the price of his product when the customer is concerned about its reliability will be addressing the wrong concern. This will only emotionally confuse the customer. Often people are not confident enough to directly express what's on their mind. Sometimes you have to use gentle probing questions to get to the heart of their real concerns.

Again, questions should not be manipulative or used as a weapon against another party. You use questions to find their concerns and to address them. Professional speakers who present to hundreds or thousands of people at a time use the acronym *WIIFM* to describe this factor. People listen to speakers with this subconscious thought:

What's in it for me? It's human nature to be concerned with one's own welfare. If you accept this characteristic as a fact and adjust your message accordingly, your communication will have a greater impact.

It should be apparent by now that the goal in effective communication is *understanding*. You listen not just to hear the words of the other person, but also to perceive the meaning behind the words. Understanding is so important that Stephen Covey made it one of his *7 Habits of Highly Effective People*—"Habit #5: Seek First to Understand, Then to Be Understood." Understanding in communication comes from *hearing* the words, *knowing* the person, and *looking* for feedback.

What is feedback? It's the most important aspect of two-way communication. Covey's habit has two parts, first to understand, and then to be understood. You can be skillful at the first, which will pay great dividends. However, if you neglect the second part, being understood, then true communication is not occurring. Feedback is information that each person provides the other to indicate that their communication is accurate.

For example, a simple "I understand" is feedback telling you that the other person comprehends what you are saying. Words alone, however, are not enough. Everyone is guilty at some time of saying that they understand something when they really don't. One way that you can indicate to the other person that you truly understand them (because you're carefully listening, right?) is to repeat what the other person has said back to them, except you rephrase it to reflect the underlying emotion.

For example, if you are a salesperson and your customer makes a comment about the warranty, you might say, "I understand that with a purchase like this you might be concerned about reliability. Let me reassure you that ..." This is a simple example, and of course the specifics of each conversation will demand an appropriate response. What's important is that you address the underlying emotions and concerns of the other party, and that you not simply say the words "I understand" when you really don't.

You also need to look for nonverbal clues that indicate the other party understands you. When the other person nods his or her head, for example, it can mean that he or she agrees with what you are saying. On the other hand, if the other person avoids making eye contact, it can mean that he or she disagrees or is uncomfortable with what you are saying.

No one of these indicators is 100 percent accurate all the time. They have to be put together like a jigsaw puzzle during the communication, using your knowledge of the person and the situation to arrive at the proper communication method. Good communicators adjust their message so that they achieve the most effective communication with each individual. Adaptability and awareness are the key attributes when you seek to improve your own communication.

The most accurate form of feedback, of course, is the result you obtain from your communication. Your goal is always to communicate in ways that keeps everyone on purpose, that is, in the words of an old folk song, they keep their "eyes on the prize." If you are not getting the results you want, then you need to adjust your communication. Obtaining the final product, the goal of your message, is the truest indication of success that you can have.

Remember this important feature of communication that many of us have trouble remembering: *good communication is not a monologue.* Most of us don't truly listen when another person is speaking. We usually are thinking about how to respond.

Two-way communication is the best way to get the results you want and to ensure accuracy in the exchange. Misunderstandings can be eliminated quickly, if they occur at all. Listening to the other person helps you improve your own side of the conversation. It also helps you recognize and eliminate static.

Static is anything that gets in the way of your message. It could be something as fundamental as not having an accurate grasp of a situation. You could be trying to have the wrong conversation—the other person's concerns might be emotional, while you are trying to convey factual information. In either case, you're not speaking the right language.

Knowing your audience will help ensure that you are communicating the right message. If static is something impeding your message, then sending the wrong message is static on steroids. If you have a purpose for your communication, then your message needs to fit your purpose. It's simply a waste of energy to work at skillfully communicating the wrong message.

Establishing Relationships

In all communications, whether an intimate conversation with a close friend or a mass email to your entire company, you are establishing relationships. Even with strangers, you are shaping the bond that you share for the moment of your communication. Something as simple as holding a door open for a stranger tells them a bit about you. With those associates whom you deal with many times a day, the relationship is stronger, formed by the many threads of communication that you engage in.

I've used the word *skill* throughout this chapter for a reason. Communicating well is something that you can work on and develop. Like any other skill, of course, you have to be willing to put in the time and effort to improve. Plus, as with any skill that deals with other people and relationships, you never stop learning. Constant improvement is your goal in communicating. You know that you will never be perfect, that you will make mistakes along the way, but you also realize that you are doing the best you can and that your intentions are honorable.

Many people join organizations such as Toastmasters or Dale Carnegie to improve their communication skills. As I have emphasized this entire chapter, communicating is more than simply speaking. These organizations provide opportunities for you to learn about relating with other people, the key skill to real, effective communication. Look for local resources for these organizations in the Yellow Pages or online. The website for Toastmasters International is http://www.toastmasters.org, and you can learn more about Dale Carnegie seminars at http://www. dalecarnegie.com.

There are a variety of ways to study communication, but they all require your awareness of how they apply to the relationships you want to form. Be sincere and honest in your dealings with others—be the type of person you ask others to be—and that will communicate more to others than anything you say. Your ability to communicate with other people and the relationships you build will determine the level of your success.

Okay, let's take a breath. Here is a quick recap:

- You've chosen a vision of your success.

- You've created a goal statement.

- You're actively using your twin engines: Inner-Forming™ and Outer-Performing™.

- You're communicating and developing relationships with others.

- You're moving right along toward your goals.

Now let's suppose that you have been working toward your goal for a period of time and you're not seeing any good results yet. This may cause you to doubt your ability to achieve your goals. Or maybe you've taken some massive action, and you experienced a failure. This too may cause you to doubt. In either case it may cross your mind to forget all this nonsense about achieving your goals and just quit. If this happens, it's a very important moment that we will discuss in the next chapter.

10
The Art of Not Giving Up

Effort only fully releases its reward

after a person refuses to quit.

—Napoleon Hill

As much as any of us would like to believe that we are unique—and we are, in many and varied ways—there is no need to use unique methods to achieve success. Many people throughout the ages have been successful, and their methods and characteristics are there for us to imitate. The laws of success, like the laws of physics, apply to everyone. If you throw an apple into the air, it will come down, obeying the law of gravity. If you use the methods of successful people, you will also be successful.

Successful people, like any other group, have a variety of characteristics. Most of them are talented in some way—professional athletes are physically gifted. Some are very intelligent or have a talent for communicating or influencing people. They are complex human beings, just like the rest of us. However, every successful person shares one attribute, and that attribute is the key to their success.

What is that key to success? *Persistence.* As in the quote from Calvin Coolidge I mentioned earlier, "Nothing in the world can take the place of persistence." It's precisely that simple. Persistence is simply the art of not giving up. There are few concepts in the world as simple to understand but as hard to execute as moving toward your goal no matter how hard it gets.

Think about it. The other attributes without persistence don't amount to much. You can be intelligent, physically gifted, and educated, and still wind up lost, working at a job you hate, and completely unsure about what you should be doing to improve your life. It's only through having a plan and possessing the toughness to work through hard times that you can truly reach success.

Especially for those who are talented or gifted in some area, lacking persistence and determination can be frustrating. Often things in life come easily for such people—at least when they are young. Our schools reward these people with good grades or acclaim for their athletic feats. Talented people often breeze through school without ever having to crack a book or do an extra workout.

As adults, however, life can be harsh. Smart people run into subjects that they can't grasp, and they have never developed the work habits they need to master a tough subject. High school athletes earn athletic scholarships to universities where the level of competition is much higher, and they lack the discipline to excel, often losing those scholarships. In such cases, without the rigors of hard work to temper their skills, talented people give up, never taking advantage of the gifts they were given.

Consider, on the other hand, those marginal students or athletes who had to struggle to make good grades or earn a spot on the first string. Through extra study and hard work, they learned the art of persistence. They recognize that they can overcome adversity through determination, and they know that if they simply keep on working, they can break through and achieve their goals.

Persistence alone doesn't guarantee success, of course. Compassion and awareness are requirements for anyone who aspires to the highest levels of success. Persistence without awareness is simply stubbornness. Awareness makes it possible for a determined person to adjust his or her methods while still moving forward. Without persistence, he or she would give up.

A persistent person needs compassion so that he or she doesn't use determination as an excuse to step on other people as he or she pursues a goal. Success, as we have learned, means working *with* other people, not trampling them in your desire to succeed. Persistence without compassion is simply arrogance.

What Exactly Is Persistence?

The dictionary defines persistence as "to continue steadfastly or firmly in some purpose or course of action, especially in spite of opposition." It doesn't take much persistence to achieve something that's easy. That's why so many people can do it. The most successful people do the things that less successful people won't do. It's in the face of opposition that persistence pays off.

What the dictionary can't define is the strength inside a person that makes them refuse to quit. When the Apollo 13 space mission suffered an explosion that destroyed their effort to reach the moon and threatened to kill the crew, flight director Gene Krantz refused to give up. Against nearly impossible odds, Kranz and his team refused to quit until they had the crew safely back on Earth.

When the explosion ruined their chance to reach the moon, Kranz recognized that they had a new mission: the rescue of the crew. His persistence and determination forced the ground team to come up with improbable ways to filter the air in the space capsule and to get the crew back to Earth, despite the loss of most of their rocket boosters' power.

Very few of us have the task of solving such a high-profile problem, but most of us are forced to deal with pressure that is just as damaging—pressure from our peers and close relationships to conform. Tackling an abstract problem in space technology sometimes seems simple compared to having to face our family's disapproval.

Persistence, then, is the refusal to quit, to exercise a hard inner core that keeps you on track despite the difficulties you encounter. That inner strength comes from having to be persistent again and again, working against the odds over the years.

Why is persistence so important? For one thing, without persistence doubt creeps in. If you have been in tough situations before, then you know that with determination and effort you are able to overcome obstacles. You have been tested and tried and have still been able to achieve your goals, despite setbacks and resistance. Proven persistence helps harden your resolve.

Without persistence, you're never really sure if you'll be able to achieve something or not. You may decide to only give it a "good try." You may decide that it's simply too hard to succeed, and that it is not worth the effort. Doubt makes cowards of us all.

Without persistence, it's easier to fall behind and to lose all of the progress that you've made thus far. It's human nature to want to do the easy thing, but if you make the easy choice every time, you're less likely to achieve success. Successful people do the difficult things that unsuccessful people fail to do. Only when you have the inner drive that tells you nothing is going to stop you from reaching your goal are you able to go the extra mile and succeed.

Don't forget as part of your Inner-Forming˜ to see yourself as a very persistent person, handling situations like a leader and getting stronger and stronger when faced with challenges.

Someone who is persistent doesn't necessarily look for the "big win." Success is rarely achieved in one big bite. Those with persistence know that if you keep tapping on a brick wall with a small hammer, a crack will eventually form, and once the crack is formed then the whole wall can come down. It's possible to eat an entire elephant if you simply take it one bite at a time.

What matters is the goal, not all the distractions, obstacles, or hindrances that occur along the way. While trying to achieve anything worthwhile, these kinds of things are bound to happen. If you have developed persistence, you know and expect these things to happen. You prepare yourself mentally, and when a problem occurs you're not surprised. You simply take it in stride as part of the process of achieving the success that you have been working so hard to find.

What really matters—what's more important than any discomfort you suffer along the way—is the goal.

Persistence, then, is vitally important. How do you go about developing persistence? The key is to start small. That's why learning persistence as a child is so useful; most of the things that you're asked to do and most of the things that you attempt as a child are simple and small. Your self-image and self-worth are not caught up in whether you succeed or not.

When working to develop your persistence, then, start with small projects that have bothered you because you have faced difficulties you were unable to overcome, at least up until now. Choose a small project and determine that you're going to finish it, regardless of what it takes. Whether it's finishing a woodworking project or completing a difficult crossword puzzle, determine that you are going to finish. Make this promise to yourself and treat it as though you had made it to someone else. Then keep your promise.

Downplay Problems

Another habit that you can develop to learn persistence is to stop making mountains out of molehills. In other words, don't make problems larger than they really are. In fact, you should do just the opposite. If a problem or an obstacle is at a difficulty level of eight out of ten, talk about it and treat it as though it were a level two. This doesn't mean that you don't make the effort to overcome the obstacle. What you're doing, though, is training your subconscious mind to treat the difficulty as solvable.

When you minimize obstacles, you are playing a psychological trick on your subconscious. Remember, the subconscious mind believes everything it's told. Whether you magnify the problem or minimize it, your subconscious mind will accept it as true. When the problem is presented as impossible to solve, the subconscious mind limits the amount of imagination and creativity that it will devote to solving the problem. When a problem is presented as minor, however, the subconscious mind will allocate whatever resources necessary to solve the problem. What you're doing is removing the limits on your own mind.

To develop persistence you may have to overcome a lifetime of conditioning. Success doesn't come easily or without a price. The traits—such as persistence—necessary to achieve success are the results of making hard decisions and doing what needs to be done. In today's society, such traits are uncommon. Because of this, most of the people you know or are related to don't understand the persistence needed to achieve your goals.

There's a story about researchers who put a group of monkeys in a room. In the middle of the room was a pole. At the top of the pole hung a bunch of bananas. One at a time, each monkey tried to climb the pole to get the bananas. Each time a monkey tried to climb the pole, the researchers would use a fire hose to hit the monkey with a blast of water that knocked him off the pole. Each of the monkeys tried to climb the pole, and each was knocked off by the blast.

Eventually, they all quit trying to climb the pole. The experimenters then replaced one of the monkeys with a different one that didn't know about the hose and the water. When he tried to climb the pole, the other monkeys pulled him down. One at a time, each of the monkeys was replaced until finally the room was full of monkeys that had never been hit by the blast of water. None of them would climb the pole to get the bananas, but none of them knew why. They were only acting as they had been taught.

Momentum

You may be familiar with the term *momentum*. In elections one candidate or another may be described as "having momentum." In a ball game, announcers might say that a team has momentum. In regard to your success, it's almost impossible to succeed without momentum. It's such an important aspect that once you have it, you have to fight hard to keep it because it's very difficult to get back.

What is momentum? The standard short definition is "force or speed of movement." In the physical world, it's easy to observe momentum as a bike rolling downhill or a snowball or avalanche increasing speed as it goes downhill. In cartoons, a snowball gets bigger and bigger until it's often the size of a house (usually with someone rolled up inside).

Momentum works in this case because the object has an ever-increasing amount of mass gathering behind it as it moves. The avalanche gathers more snow behind it until it sometimes takes down a whole mountainside. Similarly, a bicycle gathers speed because of the force of gravity and its constant pull on the bike.

In either case, momentum means increasing the speed of movement. With an avalanche, it's downhill. With success, the momentum is what sends you upward. Success depends on progress, and progress is defined by movement. You can't be considered successful if you are always stuck in one place. Almost by definition, success means moving from one place to another. This may not be physical movement, but you are moving to a higher level in your life and outlook.

As part of the process of success, you will move from one point to another. When you practiced goal-setting earlier, you likely established subgoals that moved you progressively closer to your larger goal. This is the way the process works, and without movement there is no way for you to attain momentum—hence the definition, "force or speed of *movement*."

This description of physical momentum can apply to the momentum of success also. You have to have force to move past your obstacles. This force is embodied in the persistence you show as you work toward your goal. This force gives you the ability to overcome such obstacles and to move to the next level of accomplishment.

You attain speed in your momentum as you move closer to your goal. With few exceptions, success begets success, and the more successful habits you practice and demonstrate, the faster success seems to appear. Ask any wealthy person about their millions and they'll tell you that the first million dollars was the hardest to earn.

Inertia

If you study momentum, then you have to learn about inertia. Just as momentum is the speed and force of movement, inertia is defined as the characteristic of a body at rest to tend to stay at rest. In human terms, we know it as being a couch potato or as apathy.

There are always forces that try to keep you motionless, unable to move. Whether it's family pressure, peer pressure, or a load of guilt that someone has tried to put on you because you're trying to improve your life, the force of inertia is very powerful indeed. It takes a tremendous amount of psychological strength and energy to make the changes you want to make to achieve your success— although practicing your Inner-Forming" effectively makes everything a whole lot easier.

One very common pressure to keep you in your place is the "paralysis of analysis." Earlier I recommended that you think before you act. Some people use this as an excuse to keep from ever acting. They will try to think something through all the way to its end, even if the matter is so complex that there is no way to see the end. They will wait to take any action until conditions are absolutely perfect—and that time never comes.

This type of inertia is easy to rationalize. You simply tell yourself that you are "thinking it through" properly because you don't want to waste any effort. Deep down, however, you know the truth— you're trying to escape taking that first step. Sometimes all you can do is plan as carefully as is prudent, and then act without knowing how something is going to end.

There's nothing wrong with this. Football coaches know that despite working for hours on perfecting their plays, only 10 percent or so work out as they are designed. The other 90 percent of the time someone gets hurt, a team gets outplayed in a particular position, or it's raining and they can't hold onto the ball. That's why coaches design more than one play for their playbook. They know they will have to adapt to new conditions as the game progresses.

In the same way, you can think a plan through as well as possible but then be ready to adapt to changing conditions. If you refuse to take any action unless you can see it through to a perfect and inevitable end, then you are doomed to never take any action.

The hardest part of gaining any momentum is to get moving in the first place. Rocket scientists know that more than 90 percent of the fuel expended in launching a rocket is spent lifting it the first few inches off the ground. Once the vessel is moving, it becomes easier and easier to lift. Once it has escaped Earth's gravity, it takes almost no fuel to guide the vessel.

In this same way, you will expend the greatest amount of effort in moving from being an inert object to a moving, successful person. Overcoming the urge to do nothing is the greatest exertion of will power in your journey toward success. The good news is that once you get started, your momentum will increase and become easier for you to maintain.

Momentum is important because success requires movement. Success is built around action and activity, both words that indicate something moving or happening. If you don't move, then nothing happens.

Developing Momentum

How do you develop momentum? Simply get started. You don't wait for the perfect plan or perfect conditions. You take a prudent look at the situation, make the best decision you can, and then act. This requires accessing your inner power, the internal essence that makes you the person you are. Your abilities are far greater than you imagine, and you can only show them if you dig down deep and get started.

Once you have made the decision to move—the hardest decision you may ever make in your life—then you have to figure out how to move ahead most effectively. In management theory there is a concept called "force field analysis." This concept means that in keeping a situation static or unmoving, there is equal pressure from both *driving forces* and *restraining forces*. Driving forces move you toward taking action, while restraining forces prevent you from taking action.

A driving force would be your desire to achieve success. A restraining force would be peer pressure to keep you where you are. For you to make progress, you have to either increase the driving force or reduce the restraining force. I advise spending slightly more effort removing restraining forces than adding to the driving forces. The exact percentage is not important, but for discussion let's say 60 percent to 40 percent

The nature of many restraining forces resembles a metal spring. The more you push against them, the more compact and inflexible they can become. Eventually the pressure is so great that they can't be pushed any further. It's far easier to remove the force than to keep pushing against it.

Many problems you will face will involve other people. Many times they won't understand your desire for success and the change that it requires. They have become comfortable with keeping you in a particular box, and they want to keep you inside that box. Negative thinkers will tell you that what you want to achieve is impossible. They may even become angry at your desire to reach your dream.

If you care for other people, then also care for those who want to keep you where you are. Retain your trustworthiness by keeping your promises to them. Most of all, be conscious and aware of their fears, and do your best to reassure them. They may not come around to supporting you fully, but you will have done what you needed to do to assuage their fears and concerns.

To maintain your momentum, constantly feed your inner strength. Remember that your Inner-Forming" is absolutely key here. Remain aware of obstacles and potential rough spots—your awareness will make the journey smoother. You also feed your inner strength by creating a successful environment for yourself—positive people and a positive atmosphere are vital. The drive to succeed is like a plant in your soul, one that's very hardy but also needs attention. Give it the proper care and nurturing it requires to thrive.

Remember: persistence, momentum, and inertia. Inertia keeps you in the same place. Momentum gets you moving. Persistence keeps you moving when things get tough.

Case Studies

Sometimes it helps to discover other people who have achieved success or overcome obstacles. Here are a few case studies that you may find enlightening.

Jerry

Jerry was the kind of guy who was always in a good mood and always had something positive to say. He was a restaurant manager, and whenever he changed jobs, his employees eventually wound up following into his new job because he was such a joy to work with. Whenever you asked him how he was, he would say, "If I were any better, I'd be twins!"

One day I went up to Jerry and asked him, "How can you be positive all the time?"

Jerry said, "Each morning I wake up, and I have two choices. One, I can choose to be in a good mood, or two, I can choose to be in a bad mood. I simply make the choice to be in a good mood each day. If something bad happens, I can choose to be a victim or I can learn from it."

One night after the rest of the employees had left the restaurant, robbers came in and held up Jerry. They ordered him to open the safe, but he was so nervous that his trembling fingers couldn't work the combination. The robbers grew angry and shot him. Fortunately, Jerry was found quickly and rushed to the hospital.

After many surgeries, Jerry was eventually released. Several months later, I talked to him and asked how he was doing. He said, "If I were any better, I'd be twins." I asked him how, given the horrible situation that he'd gone through, he could have such a positive outlook.

Jerry said, "When the paramedics were taking me in the ambulance, they kept telling me how well I was doing, that I was going to be all right. But in their eyes, I saw that they doubted I was going to make it. When they wheeled me into surgery, the nurse was asking me all the typical questions before they did the procedure. She asked me if I was allergic to anything and I said, "Bullets!" I told them, "I choose to live. Please operate on me as if I were alive, not dead."

Liviu Librescu

In 2007, a mentally disturbed student went on a shooting rampage at Virginia Polytechnic Institute (Virginia Tech). His attack left 32 dead and over two dozen wounded. The death toll would have been much higher if not for the bravery of a mechanics and engineering professor who threw himself in front of the door of his classroom when the shooter tried to enter. He held the door long enough for all of the students in the room to escape through the windows. What is remarkable about this story is that the professor was 76-year-old Liviu Librescu, a survivor of the Holocaust. After surviving the horrors of a concentration camp, Librescu sacrificed himself to save his students.

Edmund Hillary

Edmund Hillary was the first man to climb Mount Everest, the highest mountain in the world. He reached the peak in 1953. The remarkable thing about Hillary's feat is that he had unsuccessfully tried to climb Mount Everest in 1952. After the 1952 attempt, Hillary was invited to speak to a group in England. He received thunderous applause as he walked to the stage. Instead of addressing the audience, though, he pointed to a picture of the mountain and said in a loud voice, "Mount Everest, you beat me the first time, but I'll beat you the next time, because you've grown all you're going to grow. *But I'm still growing.*"

11
The Oracle

Human beings, who are almost unique in having
the ability to learn from the experience of others,
are also remarkable for their apparent disinclination to do so.

—Douglas Adams

In ancient times rulers of lands would consult with an *oracle* for guidance. The oracle—a source of wise counsel, often spiritual in nature—dispensed advice and wisdom. It's comforting to know that in our modern society there are still sources of wisdom. The sources of wisdom, however, are not always found in schools. *Wisdom* is different from *knowledge*.

If you want to learn something, you have a lot of choices. You can learn on your own. With the advent of the Internet, there is more information available to you than ever before. You only need a computer and you can pull up information on every topic imaginable. Use Google or some other search engine and you are on your way to being self-educated.

However, there is a problem with this type of learning in regard to your success. It's possible that you will accumulate a lot of information without actually being *educated*. What's the point of learning a lot of facts that turn out not to have any bearing on what you want to achieve? After all, if you had that knowledge—*when* to apply particular information—then you would already be educated.

Learning by yourself, then, for those who are so inclined, can help you gather information, but it can't give you judgment. Without some sort of guidance, you may waste most of your time on details that are not pertinent.

The Socratic Method

There is another method of learning called the *Socratic method*. It's based on the principle of asking questions. The point of the questions is to illustrate any weak points in the other person's argument or presentation of facts. By doing this, you help the person strengthen his or her argument, which will lead to better understanding of the subject.

The Socratic method is great when a student has had an opportunity to learn about the subject on his own, either in class or independent study. The instructor asks open-ended questions, letting the student assimilate the answers he gives into his learning. By having to articulate answers to a series of questions, the student deepens his knowledge and grasp of the subject.

The point of this discussion of the Socratic method is that when you engage in conversation with someone who knows more about a subject than you do, the questions that arise often lead you to discover answers yourself. You know more than you think you know, and being able to find and articulate answers helps ensure that the information becomes a permanent part of your warehouse of knowledge.

When learning about success, you want to learn from someone who has achieved what you want to. Without that type of teacher, you don't know for sure if what you are learning is accurate or useful. The Socratic method of learning is fantastic when done with someone who is knowledgeable in the subject you want to know. When done by someone unfamiliar with your subject, the Socratic method can still deepen your knowledge, but with less effect. After all, the instructor doesn't know for sure what questions to ask that will provide the best result.

A Mentor

What you are looking for here is someone who has the knowledge and experience in your area of interest. You want someone who has demonstrated success and is readily available to you so that you can have ongoing conversations in which you ask and answer questions, thus deepening your knowledge. This ideal person is called a *mentor*.

The word *mentor* originally comes from Greek mythology. When Odysseus left for the Trojan War, he left his trusted friend Mentor in charge of his son Telemachus.

In modern terms, a mentor is an experienced person who serves as a trusted counselor and advisor. This definition dovetails nicely with the definition of oracle. You are looking for wise counsel when you consult with your mentor. With expertise in your subject area and being available to answer questions, a mentor is a combination of the best elements of other ways of learning. Having the proper mentor in your corner will accelerate your success like nothing else.

When you seek out a mentor, you are looking for someone who has done what you want to accomplish in a particular area. You may remember from goal-setting that you have different goals for different areas of your life. A mentor may have great expertise in one area but almost none in another area. It's important that your mentor have the knowledge you want in the area in which you need help.

For example, you may want to improve your relationship with your spouse or significant other. You wouldn't necessarily want to take relationship advice from a successful businessman who is four-times divorced. His expertise obviously lies in another area! Instead, a person who is in a healthy, happy relationship might be more useful in this particular area. Leave the businessman for another area.

Your mentor will also be someone who has done what you want to do—they have walked the walk.

The ideal mentor will also be a motivated teacher—not necessarily in the professional sense (with a teaching certificate), but someone who is interested in sharing their knowledge. Most people with experience are happy to share what they've learned along the way, and are sometimes flattered by the request to mentor you. They know that by sharing their knowledge they are leaving behind something that will outlast them.

There are many specific ways a mentor can help you succeed. Here are just a few examples. A mentor can

- give you advice or suggestions on how to handle specific situations

- help draw out your strengths

- help manage and eliminate your weaknesses

- help you with goal-setting
- help you develop your plan of action
- introduce you to the right people or businesses

Finding the Right Mentor

How do you go about finding the right mentor? As with everything else in your quest for success, you have to be aware. Awareness is a trait you want to develop and display at every step. In this case, awareness means observing your world and being able to see what's going on around you. You need to be well-informed to find the right mentor.

First of all, of course, you need to know what area you want to be mentored in. Is it in relationships, health, career, fitness, or finances? When you know the particular area you want help in, then it narrows the field of people whom you are looking at for help. At this point, listen to your friends or partners to get their opinion of someone who is adept in your area of interest.

Besides listening to others, you can also read newspapers, watch television, and read trade journals to find those who are accomplished in your particular field. Staying informed means that you become an expert about a subject. Note that I didn't say an expert *in* the subject, but you'll be someone who knows enough to judge expertise in others.

I'm a great believer in the idea of solving a problem or answering a question in the simplest manner possible. When looking for a mentor, look to those close to you first. The ideal mentor may be a relative, a neighbor, or someone in your town. Geographic proximity is a great advantage in a mentoring relationship. It provides immediate contact and enables you to have more frequent face-to-face conversations.

For many people, though, the ideal mentor is not someone close. Especially in business matters, the ideal mentor may be in another city or even another country. A hundred years ago, mentoring relationships were often conducted by correspondence. The advantage of this type of relationship was that people of the early twentieth-century were expert letter writers. Often their correspondence was thoughtful, well-organized, and contained prose that was almost poetry. The only disadvantage was distance.

Luckily, communication has never been easier. Using the Internet, email, cell phones, text messaging, or online chat can make meeting with your mentor almost as effective as having lunch with them. You are no longer restricted by distance. However, keep in mind the art of correspondence that our ancestors showed. Use the latest technology with the same elegance that our grandparents and great-grandparents showed in their letters.

Once you have found the proper person to be your mentor, how do you go about establishing a mentoring relationship? First of all, respect the person whom you approach. That person may have limits on time or their desire to be a mentor. Don't approach them with the idea that you can force someone to be your mentor. As useful as their knowledge and experience might be, it dilutes their effectiveness to you if they feel pressured to do something they don't want to do.

On the other hand, if you can demonstrate how such a relationship might be beneficial to them, then do so. In the ideal mentoring relationship, both of you feel as though you have profited from the exchange. You have gained knowledge and information from the mentor, and he or she has gained satisfaction in helping you.

Of course, there may be more tangible benefits to the mentor, as well. Financial advisor Dave Ramsey has said that when he was trying to learn about how finances work in the real world, he never hesitated to buy lunch for a millionaire who was willing to talk to him. A millionaire could probably afford the lunch more than you, but it's a nice gesture to pick up the check if you are there to learn from the other person.

While you don't want to coerce or force a person to be your mentor, it is important that you exhibit a desire and passion for your subject. You can't approach this situation as simply another "assignment" you're required to do to be successful. No one wants to be around someone who lacks passion for their subject.

Think about it. Imagine you were an expert in a special area, let's say archery. Someone approaches you to be their mentor. When you talk to them, you find that they don't really care anything about archery, bows, arrows, or targets. They are only there to talk to you because they think they need to. How would you feel?

By communicating your passion for your subject, you show respect for the mentor and what he knows. If the subject is important enough for you to seek out a mentor, then you already feel passion—you simply need to show it. The right mentor will appreciate your honest desire to learn from him or her.

The Mentoring Relationship

Earlier I mentioned that in the mentoring relationship, each of you benefit. This is a concept known as *reciprocity*. The mentoring relationship is a mutual exchange of value for value. You, of course, are benefiting by gaining knowledge from your mentor. What you must do is find what is of value to your mentor.

In some cases you may have information or knowledge that can benefit your mentor. Even in his area of expertise, you may have an outlook or viewpoint that is of importance. Older mentors may value the judgments of a younger person simply to get that person's opinion. A truly successful person never quits learning, and hearing another person's viewpoint—especially if that viewpoint is much different from their own—is sometimes of great value.

The passion and desire you show may also be of value to the mentor. Sometimes a person has a lot of experience in an area, but no longer feels the same fire he or she did when first starting out. By associating with you, your mentor may feel the drive and passion that he or she had when he or she was younger, and that fire may be what he or she needs to reach even higher levels of success. This is yet another reason why you should communicate your desire and passion to your mentor.

Remember that in the mentoring relationship you are part of the process. You have to remain involved and participate. If you approach the task as though the mentor is a servant who is there to dish out knowledge without any commitment on your part, then you have the wrong mind-set. Each of you is there to benefit the other in some way, and you will abuse the relationship if you try to take advantage of it.

Historically, the best learning has always been achieved with the help of a mentor. A rounded education is best accomplished through first benefiting from the wisdom and experience of a mentor, and then serving as a mentor to someone else. Plato served as a mentor to Aristotle, who then served as a mentor to Alexander the Great. This is the cycle of education that civilization has developed.

Having a mentor can boost your confidence like nothing else and can give you a huge advantage when avoiding potential problems. But before we talk about how to handle setbacks, let's discuss another powerful concept that will help you avoid problems.

Mastermind Groups

Call me kooky, but I like the idea of preventing problems from happening in the first place. Honestly speaking, your Inner-Forming¨ helps you accomplish this to a large extent by keeping you moving in a straight line toward your goal, thereby avoiding useless side roads where it's easy to get sidetracked or lost. Of course, you'll most likely have some problems, but avoiding many of them, especially big ones, will make your life a lot easier.

A great way to avoid problems and speed up your success at the same time is to take advantage of the *mastermind* concept, where a group of unique individuals join forces to create solutions, ideas, and action plans for each of its members.

Sometimes known as a "goals club," a mastermind group is not formed with the same type of goals as civic clubs or service organizations. The mastermind group is formed specifically to provide synergy so that each member benefits in his or her own way, helping each member move toward his or her goals.

A mastermind group may have any number of members and may last for an indefinite time. It is a loosely-organized way to focus energy on a particular task or project, bringing the expertise and energy of everyone involved to bear on the matter. Everyone involved becomes more self-aware, and the social pressure of the group makes it possible for everyone involved to work more effectively.

Working in a mastermind group makes it possible to associate with like-minded people to develop action plans. Usually not simply a think tank, the mastermind group is looking for results. Creativity and ideas are stimulated from the synergistic nature of the group.

To get the most out of a mastermind group, you first have to find like-minded people who have the same dedication to success that you do. While they may not share your particular goals, they all have the goal of achieving success. Once you have found another person (or, if you're lucky, several people) who share that drive for success, you need to participate by sharing ideas, suggestions, and encouragement with the other members. There are no "paper members" in a mastermind group as everyone is expected to participate equally. Each person brings different strengths to the group, so everyone must stay involved to make the group successful.

You also have to understand the mission of the group. This mission is to maximize the success of each individual by helping each other develop sound plans of action. It's always pleasant to have social interactions; however, this is a secondary results and is not the overall mission of the group. Sometimes, unfortunately, due to poor communication, the mission gets garbled. It helps to periodically remind everyone involved of what they are there to accomplish.

When you participate in a mastermind group, you have to approach it with an open mind. To gain the most benefit from the group, you have to be willing to learn, which means being flexible enough to listen to the idea of others. You may feel as though your idea is the best—and it may be—but you won't know that until you have given due consideration to the ideas of other people.

Brainstorming

Participating in a mastermind group will likely involve brainstorming sessions. Brainstorming is when a group of people generate ideas on how to resolve a particular issue. The concept gets its name from the "storm" of ideas that accompany a good session. Everyone who is involved participates and has an equal say in the generation of ideas. Although one person usually has to serve as a sort of ringmaster to keep the circus from getting out of control, this atmosphere of controlled chaos is what generates the best ideas.

While there has to be some direction, in a good brainstorming session there is no judgment of ideas while they are being generated. Sometimes what at first looks like a ridiculous idea turns out to be the best solution. The ringmaster has to make sure that no person's ideas are devalued by someone else in the group.

It's also important to write down the ideas that are generated. This is often on a board in front of the group or in some other way where the ideas are visible to all. In a good session, there will be too many ideas generated to remember them all. Sometimes, the proximity of two ideas leads to another idea, creating an amalgam of ideas already presented.

Brainstorming is beneficial because it stimulates creative solutions to problems and creative answers to questions. The almost crazy atmosphere that occurs in the best brainstorming sessions leads people to come up with unique and innovative ideas. The looseness works to make everyone comfortable enough to provide great answers.

For a brainstorming session to be effective, there should be a few ground rules. First, no idea is to be judged when it's first presented. An idea may require further development to be viable, but that might not be known at first sight. Prejudging kills the creative atmosphere, as someone whose idea has been prematurely shot down may be reluctant to participate afterward.

It also helps to have a very specific objective in the session. When ideas can be addressed narrowly, it makes workable solutions more likely. An overly broad subject leads to ideas that are all over the place. A free flow of ideas is the goal, not a giant number of inapplicable solutions.

After the ideas have been generated, they can be looked at with a fresh eye to determine which ones have potential and which ones might need to be tweaked to make them work. Judgment is reserved until this time, and then only after discussion within the group. This judgmental period is separate from the idea-generating period. The people who offered ideas have a chance to explain their ideas and smooth out what they offered during the session. This discussion is often what leads to new, unlikely solutions.

Successful and wise people regularly make use of mentors, mastermind groups, and brainstorming sessions. These methods really help thrust a person toward his or her goal.

In my own life, I am grateful that I've been able to benefit enormously from these types of groups. I belong to several. Some are with good friends, while others are with strategic business alliance partners.

Join groups and surround yourself with people who share your commitment to improvement and who understand what you're trying to do. There is no benefit to trying to go on the journey of success alone. Other people can recharge your batteries with their own energy and passion. Eliminate those people who are negative or who try to divert you from your goals.

Mentors and mastermind groups can help lift you higher than you can go by yourself. But even with the help of others, the truth is that you will inevitably have to face *some* problems alone. It's just not possible to avoid all of them, even if you have a mentor and a mastermind group. But, it is possible to handle problems and setbacks in the right manner so they can actually increase your momentum.

12
Falling Then Rising

When written in Chinese, the word "crisis" is composed of two characters—one represents danger, and the other represents opportunity.

—John F. Kennedy

In a perfect world, a chart of your progress toward your goal would be a smooth, upward line that ended with the gold star that marked "success." Unfortunately, the world is not perfect, and your progress won't be that smooth. Too many factors combine to prevent solid success.

You are, after all, only human. By nature, humans are vulnerable. Sometimes you can make mistakes that will take you all the way back to the beginning of your journey. This is frustrating, but is a fact of life. If you recognize that mistakes happen, however, you can minimize the damage they do to you.

Why do we backslide? As I've mentioned before, it's human nature to make mistakes. That's not very comforting when you are in the middle of facing your problem. Part of the nature of a problem is that it tends to distract you from the big picture. However, even the most successful people in the world have made terrible mistakes along the way. History only remembers the successes, never the failures.

Think about writers. Ernest Hemingway is considered to be one of the greatest American authors of the twentieth century. His works are studied in writing classes and college courses. What he's remembered for, however, are a handful of novels and short stories. These few works represent only a small part of the large amount of stories and articles he wrote. What he's remembered for is the pinnacle of his success. Without taking away from his talent or reputation, let me suggest that Hemingway wrote hundreds of thousands of prose works that were less than great. In fact, I'm sure that at times he wrote things that were downright awful.

Is Hemingway remembered for his awful prose? Of course not. People know him for *The Old Man and the Sea* or *For Whom the Bell Tolls*. His style is immediately recognizable by students of literature. His mistakes and terrible efforts are forgotten and ignored.

In the same way, you will be judged by your successes, not your failures. Consider Harlan Sanders, the founder of the Kentucky Fried Chicken restaurant chain. He worked at several jobs as an adult, eventually opening a gas station where he served meals. Sanders developed a recipe and method of cooking chicken that became popular among locals. He was given the title of "Kentucky Colonel" by the governor of Kentucky and began to present himself as "Colonel Sanders."

However, Sanders's restaurant/gas station depended on traffic for its business. When the interstate opened, his traffic dropped to almost nothing, destroying his business. Colonel Sanders then had the idea of selling his chicken recipe to other restaurants. He used his Social Security check to finance his trips and eventually established a chain of restaurants that we know today as KFC.

Colonel Sanders is not the first name that comes to mind when you think of failures. However, it wasn't until age 60 that he found lasting success, and then only by virtue of a government check.

So you can see, human nature almost predestines you to backslide and have setbacks. The most successful people in history have had setbacks, but you don't always know it from the history books. Lessons are taught on their successes, not their failures.

It's also part of the law of the universe that nothing will ever go as smoothly as you think it will. The ocean has waves, roads are bumpy, and human progress often slows to a standstill. Smoothness is a man-made creation, something we look for in science fiction movies and our frying pans. Even with the best efforts, however, if you look close enough, you can see that the surface of supposedly smooth objects is still pitted and rough. The smoothness is all based on your perception.

Viewing Setbacks

How, then, should we view setbacks? It would be great if we could describe them as "backward progress" and feel better about them. Ultimately, though, we have to face the fact that setbacks place us further away from our goal than we were previously. At a time like that, how do you prevent yourself from falling into despair?

First of all, a setback is feedback. If you keep in mind that all you are getting is information, not a judgment, then it's easier to keep a setback in proper perspective. Thomas Edison, the inventor of the incandescent light bulb, worked for years to perfect a working model of his invention. The problem he had was getting proper filaments that would last long enough to create a viable commercial product.

Edison reportedly tried ten thousand different unsuccessful elements before he settled on the one that had the proper characteristics. When asked about these failures, Edison replied, "I did not fail. I found ten thousand ways that didn't work."

Use errors as feedback to correct your course. It's been said that a torpedo is sent toward its target in a straight line. By the nature of the sea—the currents and shifting conditions—the torpedo must be adjusted periodically to keep it on course. It may go too far one way, and then too far another. Eventually, however, with the adjustments, the torpedo reaches its target.

Your setbacks and mistakes are simply messages from the universe that you need to make adjustments. Sometimes the message is harsh and hard to accept. Regardless of how it feels at the time, however, you can either ignore the feedback, or you can pay attention to it and adjust your course.

Besides the message that you need to make an adjustment, setbacks can often offer you clues on what you need to do to improve. Weak spots in your process, your product, or your approach can be more precisely pinpointed when you have the benefit of suffering a setback from it. That's one thing about suffering a setback—you can completely trust the information. Nothing is as convincing as the pain of a mistake.

The Power of Habit

The key to overcoming obstacles is harnessing the *force of habit*. The classical Roman poet Ovid once said, "Nothing is more powerful than habit." Habits can benefit you or they can hurt you. A habit may be what got you into the mess you're in, and a habit may be what saves you.

What is habit? It's the execution of programming. If you are fortunate, your habit has been cultivated and you are conscious of it. Much more common, however, are habits that are based on programming from childhood or some other time in the distant past. These habits are the result of someone else's decision, not yours.

Think about something as simple as when you eat dinner. Do you have to eat at the same time each night, say 6:00 PM? Why? Is it simply a habit? If so, did you learn that habit as an adult, or do you simply eat at that time because that's what time your parents ate dinner?

Many habits are as simple as that. They are based on conditions that no longer exist. A habit of doing something in a particular way may or may not be useful in the present. You have to evaluate your habits and see if they serve a purpose.

There's the story of a young couple who had only been married a few months. One night the young bride was preparing a ham. Before she put the ham in the roasting pan, she carefully cut the ends off. After dinner, her husband commented on how good the meal was (a smart husband, he was) and asked about her habit of cutting the ends off the ham.

"That's the way my mother taught me," she replied. Curious now herself, she called her mother and asked about the technique.

"That's the way my mother taught me," said the young bride's mother.

The bride, now more curious than ever, called her grandmother and asked her about it. "Oh that," said the grandmother. "When I was a young bride, we didn't have a pan big enough to fit a whole ham, so I always cut off the ends to make it fit."

Sometimes we are cutting off the ends of the ham—following habits that may have served a purpose at one time, but are now unnecessary. Even worse, these same habits can often be detrimental, either directly working against our goals or keeping us from pursuing activities that will help us reach our goals.

Acting without thinking is not a good way to conduct your life. Habits are actions that have no conscious thought behind them. Think of the times that you have done something without realizing that you were doing it. You go through the motions of personal hygiene every morning, showering, brushing your teeth, and perhaps shaving, but when was the last time you gave conscious thought to any of these processes? After a visit to the dentist, perhaps? Or when you changed razors?

Acting without thinking—engaging in a habit—can lead to terrible setbacks. Maybe you developed the unfortunate habit of speaking harshly to vendors. After all, you're paying them, so they have to put up with your actions, right? What you don't see, however, is that by following that habit, you are creating resentment from the vendor, maybe to the point where they have favors that they could do for you, but choose not to because of how you treat them.

Ever had a salesperson offer to expedite delivery of something that you needed quickly? If you treat salespeople poorly, you haven't. Don't expect any favors from people that you mistreat. Acting like that—an unconscious mimicking of your parents perhaps, which has turned into a habit—will work against you.

As Ovid said many years ago, habit is a powerful force. Changing a habit is difficult, just ask any smoker. Experts recommend that you give yourself 30 days to change a habit. That's 30 days of paying constant attention to the conditions that cause your habit, and consciously working to change your reaction to those conditions. Thirty days of concentration is tremendously difficult, but that's the kind of effort necessary to change a habit.

As I said previously, your habits can either destroy you or they can save you. When you suffer setbacks, it's easier to believe that your habits are destroying you. That's not always the case, though. If you properly design your Inner-Forming˜ and take time every day to use the techniques, you can create new programming and new habits.

For example, let's say that your habit of overeating has led to an unhealthy weight gain. The best way to combat obesity is with diet and exercise. You may not ever exercise, but you can see the necessity of it. You can then develop the habit of exercising.

Use the techniques discussed in chapter seven. Imagine yourself being athletic and energetic. Dwell on the physical sensations of being healthy. Think about how exercising regularly and losing weight will make you feel. Then set your exercise goals and get started.

At first, you will find it extremely difficult to start exercising, especially if it's been a long time since you did it. You are overcoming inertia and trying to gain momentum. After a few days it may become a little easier, and after a couple of weeks, easier still. After a month of exercising—remember Ovid?—you will find it easier to motivate yourself to exercise.

You can do the same with any habit that you are trying to cultivate. Follow the process outlined in chapter five and set your goal to create a new, useful habit. Habits are a part of your life and can lead to setbacks. Either you control your habits, or your habits control you.

Forgive Yourself

When you make a mistake of some kind, recognize your weaknesses as a human being and exercise your right to forgive yourself. That's often much harder than it sounds, and many people find themselves incapable of doing it at all. Unless you consider yourself something better than human, however, fallibility is built into your wiring.

If you have worthy values based on positive consequences, then forgiveness is part of your outlook. If someone else wrongs you, you make the choice to forgive them. As Gandhi once said, "An eye for an eye leaves the whole world blind." You don't seek out retribution against those who have committed an error that affects you.

Why does this same spirit not apply to yourself? If you make a mistake that impedes your progress, you are merely showing a sign of being human. Forgiving yourself is a higher expression of that same humanity.

If you forgive yourself, then you can forego the process of beating yourself up unnecessarily. Honestly, expressing self-criticism and punishing yourself is a waste of energy and effort that could be put toward more productive pursuits. If you amplify your errors in conversations with other people, you are doing nothing but hurting yourself further.

That's the problem with beating yourself up over making an error: it tends to amplify the error. What was once a simple issue can become something more complicated and damaging simply because you are making it so. You are making a bad situation worse.

Even something like regret can drain your energy. Any time an emotion takes your mind off of reaching your goal, it is no longer useful. Regret is almost never useful. It's like an infection that can fester inside you, preventing you from doing anything productive. The problem with regret is that it does not lose strength as you indulge it. Regret seems to feed on itself, until your error takes on oversized proportions in your mind. Regret is a focus on the past and a blindness to the possibilities in the future.

The most important aspect of self-forgiveness is to realize that any mistakes you made were made by a past "you." The person in the past didn't have the benefit of the knowledge you gained from your mistake. Learning from your mistakes is vital if you are to make progress toward your success. You can go back and analyze the times you have made mistakes, even in the distant past, and forgive that version of you.

If you do this little exercise, don't fall into the trap of feeling regret. On the contrary, forgive yourself and move on. Be grateful for the knowledge you gained from your mistake and resolve not to repeat the mistake again.

The Trap of Perfectionism

One mistake that anyone can make is to fall into the trap of *perfectionism*. In chapter ten we talked about the problem of paralysis by analysis and how it can prevent you from taking action. On the other end of the process is perfectionism, or expecting unrealistically perfect results from your actions. Perfection is exceedingly rare, and the person who expects perfection is destined to be disappointed.

Let me make clear that there is a difference between having high expectations and perfectionism. You should always strive for excellence in whatever you do. However, being dissatisfied with anything less than perfection will inevitably lead to feelings of discouragement and lower self-worth.

One version of this type of perfectionism is to have a very specific idea of what will make you happy. The more specific your idea, the less possible it is for you to actually *be* happy. Your unspoken message is, "Only this very precise combination of conditions will make me happy. If even one element is different, I can't be happy."

Such an approach is especially damaging in relationships. If you are expecting perfect conditions in your relationships, then you are sabotaging your efforts before you even start. Relationships involve other people, and if there is one message that I have tried to make clear in this chapter, it's that human beings are imperfect. Trying to fit an inflexible template over your relationships will destroy them for sure.

When you indulge your perfectionism, you are pushing out the good for the perfect. In other words, you may have a result that is completely acceptable on all levels, yet you reject it because it doesn't fit your narrowly defined idea of perfection. Therefore, you reject a perfectly good result because it doesn't fit your template. Such a move is impractical, wasteful, and dispiriting to those around you.

The worst part of being a perfectionist is that you can never be a winner. Even with a successful result, you won't be able to resist the urge to pick at your accomplishment until you are no longer happy. "Yes, but …," you'll say, until any pleasure you can derive from winning has been completely drained away.

Getting Back on Track

If you have made a mistake, how do you go about correcting it and getting back on track? The first step is to simply recognize that you have made a mistake. Sometimes that's the most difficult part of the process. Once again, awareness plays an important role in your quest for success.

Having measurements to gauge how you are doing is useful when you want to know about a mistake quickly. Feedback from customers or partners can help. When you make an error, try to have a system in place so that you know about it as soon as possible.

After you recognize that you have made an error, accept responsibility. To others, if necessary, and definitely to yourself. If you refuse to accept responsibility for a mistake you have made, you have no choice but to play the blame game, and that is a game that has no winner. Trying to place blame on someone else drains energy from your quest and can set you back even further.

Another negative aspect of the blame game is the damage that it does to relationships. You may be able to browbeat someone into admitting that a mistake was their fault, but if it was really yours, then you will both know it and the relationship may be damaged beyond repair. Once again, stay true to your values and take responsibility when it's yours to take.

Another negative emotion is anger. Even if you don't express anger to other people, feeling it can distract you from your larger goals. This goes along with the idea of self-forgiveness—there's no point in feeling anger about something that is in the past. You can adjust your attitude so that you don't make the mistake again, but anger serves no purpose after the fact.

The most important thing about making a mistake is that you don't compound it. Learn from your mistake and move on. You need to keep your focus on your ultimate goal, and endlessly thinking over what you should have done or could have done will only make the matter worse.

No one is ever proud about making a mistake. Consequences are sometimes so severe that it's hard not to feel negative emotions about the error. But successful people know that you can't let a mistake prevent you from pursuing your ultimate goal. When you have a setback, do what you need to do to make it right. Once you have done that, you only have the future to look forward to.

13
Begin to Win

Life is full of beginnings. They are presented every day and every hour to every person. Most beginnings are small, and appear trivial and insignificant, but in reality they are the most important things in life.

—James Allen

You could read a hundred books on each of the many topics covered in this book, and it wouldn't make a difference in your life or in your chances for success. No book, video, CD, or seminar, by itself, can change your life. What matters is your personal action and personal experience. They are far more important than studying.

Many times the problem lies not in a lack of knowledge or of what to do, but the problem is knowing *where to start*. To help you with that, I have included an action guide at the back of this book. Use the action guide to figuratively build your own rocket. Follow all the steps and you'll be well on your way to making your dream a reality.

In my discussion of momentum, I mentioned that you need action in order to make things happen. Even a machine requires the action of someone flipping the switch. Getting started is the hardest part of action, and that time is now. It's time for you to get started.

A Quick Look Back

Before I give you some tips for making a quick start, let's look back at the things that you've learned:

In the first chapter, you learned about the dangers of mediocrity and what happens when you get to a particular point in your life and can't seem to move forward. Although you may have tried everything you thought you could do, you don't seem to get to the next level of success. We helped you identify where you are right now and how mediocrity spreads to every aspect of your life. This chapter is your checkup from the neck up! Sometimes it's hard to take an honest look at yourself and at how you feel about your life because you're not used to doing it, but it's really the first step on your journey—a gauge of, "What's really going on in my life?"

In chapter two we discussed the importance of thinking before you act and why simply trying harder to accomplish your goals doesn't always work. The thought (at least, effective thought) is more important than the action. We looked at self-limiting beliefs and why you may be sabotaging your progress with your thoughts. The quality of your thinking determines the quality of your actions and results. Beliefs, thoughts, and conclusions make up your mental process. By understanding this process and enhancing each part, the actions you take will be surprisingly more powerful and effective.

In chapter three I went into more detail on how the mind works and how your subconscious mind controls your life without your even realizing it. To understand what your subconscious mind is and how to change it, we discussed how it was formed over many years. From within your subconscious mind, your habits, self-image, and beliefs directly affect your behaviors and results. I introduced the concept of Inner-Forming˜ as the quickest, easiest, and most effective way to reprogram your subconscious to work for you instead of against you.

In chapter four I delved deeper into the concept of self-leadership, and how you have the power to change yourself, to choose how you will live, and ultimately how successful you will be. I encouraged you to acknowledge the awesome power within yourself and to make a decision to use it. Don't ignore it any longer. I described how your results depend on your sense of personal responsibility. Accountability is also a key ingredient to your long-term success.

In the fifth chapter, we discussed how to use the power of vision to see your own life in new and powerful ways. How would you like to live? What would you like to be? What would you like to do? When you turn off the limits you impose on your dreams and ideas, you open up new opportunities. Passion, vision, and a sense of purpose are vital to your success. We also went through the goal-setting process and how it can help you achieve your dreams. Remember, making the decision to actually achieve your vision is the real moment when your journey begins.

Chapter six is where we talked about the different outlooks and mind-sets that are important in developing your strategy. When you begin to take action, the outlook and integrity that you exude will have a big effect on your enduring success and how much help you receive from others. We examined the differences in the competitive-destructive outlook and the creative-cooperative outlook. We recognized the dangers of the scarcity mentality and the benefits of the abundance mentality.

In chapter seven we discussed how you can actually reprogram your controlling factor—your subconscious mind—to move you toward your chosen goals. Without this Inner-Forming", you won't get very far. I described visualizing your goals and self-image with as much clarity and feeling as possible, cultivating your intuitive factor, and setting your intention before acting. Doing your Inner-Forming" daily is by far the single most important habit to get into. When you design your own daily regimen of Inner-Forming" and do it properly, the physical actions you take toward your goal will have an almost magical energy behind them.

In chapter eight I described your daily physical actions as your Outer-Performing". I shared excellent ways for you to create maximum results with the least effort. Traditionally people are busy, they're always doing stuff, and yet they don't get much done. Here you learned the difference between important activities and unimportant activities. We talked about time management, as well as your daily agenda and monitoring your activity. Spending time on your continued learning is critical.

Chapter nine analyzed how effective communication is key. You're going to have to interact with other people, and they are going to play a big part in your success or your failure. We talked about congruity of message and how Gandhi encouraged you to be the change that you wish to see in the world. No one succeeds alone, and meeting the needs of others is key to getting them to follow your leadership and ultimately help you achieve your goals.

In chapter ten we focused on persistence and how to develop it. Without persistence, all the other positive attributes we've discussed won't make a big difference. You learned that by creating and maintaining your momentum, you will increase the speed of your success. You must get the ball rolling, and then keep the ball keep rolling. I also mentioned the resilience you need to be strong, even in the face of those who don't understand what you're trying to achieve.

In chapter eleven I emphasized the importance of finding the right mentor to help you achieve your goals. The right mentor can shorten your learning curve and help you move ahead. A couple sentences of good advice from your mentor could take years off your journey toward success, a fact not to be taken lightly. We also discussed the usefulness of mastermind groups and how to conduct effective brainstorming sessions.

Finally, in chapter twelve we considered the problems associated with inevitable setbacks. A setback is simply feedback. You can use setbacks as fuel for your success and allow them to make you stronger. I talked about the problems with negative emotions and the importance of self-forgiveness. I also brought up the force of habit and how it can either destroy you or save you—it's your choice.

I have deliberately selected each topic and technique covered in this book because they create amazing power for you when you use them together. Each topic energizes and reinforces the others. By using these techniques, you will grow simultaneously on many levels. In a short period of time, you'll have the personal power to command and rule your own future. This is no exaggeration!

It's not necessary that you understand how everything works before you take action. Few people know exactly how an automobile engine works, yet millions of people drive every day. *You don't have to have complete understanding before you put something to work.* Simply by going through the mechanics of the system of success, the system will begin to work for you. As you continue your Inner-Forming¨ and see the results of your actions, you will begin to have a greater comprehension of how much is possible.

Initial Ideas

With all that has been said already, it's up to you to decide what kind of life you want to lead. Have you looked at your life already? The first step in the process of reaching your goals is to create a vision of the type of success you want to achieve. Have you created such a picture? Maybe you have done more than that; maybe you have already started working on setting goals to create your vision in the physical world.

Once you have a vision and goals, it may feel like you're trying to build an entire house at once—only instead of framing, wiring, and plumbing, you're concerned with your physical health, your emotional health, your financial health, your career health, and the health of your relationships. You may not know how to make it all happen, and it's not necessary for you to know your entire plan to achieve everything you desire. In fact, if you were able to construct such a comprehensive plan, you would definitely have to change it and update it somewhere along the way because life itself changes.

The most natural way to proceed is to start with the best plan you can formulate with the knowledge you have now. Planning is a skill like any other, and the more you do it, the better you get at it. An imperfect plan is better than no plan at all.

Once you have come up with a plan, take action. A plan is lifeless until you put it into motion. Like the old saying goes, plan your work, then work your plan. It won't take long before you start seeing results.

Once you see results, you have to evaluate them to see if they are what you want. Results—points on the scoreboard—are the only measurement that counts when it comes to measuring the effectiveness of your plan. Obviously, if you get results that differ from what you intended, you have to make changes.

The ability to adapt your plan may be one of the most useful skills you can develop. We often stick with a plan well beyond the point where we know it's not working, usually out of pride or stubbornness. Making proper adjustments when they are called for makes the difference in reaching your goals. Your mentors and mastermind groups can be a huge help to you with regards to making any adjustments to your plan.

If you're not sure where to start, begin by making a short list of three to five simple things that will move you closer to your goal. These should be small things that you know you can do. The following are some examples of small steps you could take right away:

- Test drive that car you plan to own.

- Register your new business name.

- Find a success coach with whom you can work.

- Research training classes you want to take.

- Find (or start!) a mastermind group.

These are just a few examples—the possibilities are endless. Go with your intuition and feelings to determine what to do next. By developing the habit of taking action, your ability to know what to do next will improve beyond what you can ever imagine.

The actions you take should feel natural and not overly forced. If you find yourself straining—different from natural hard effort—to accomplish something, it usually means that you are going against what your instincts are telling you.

On the other hand, if you know that something is good for you, aligns with your values, and is something you should do (but you don't feel like doing it), it may be that you haven't done enough inner work. It's important to separate listening to your natural instincts from laziness, apathy, and procrastination.

It's vital that you use your intuition and feelings to examine your thoughts when it comes time to decide what to do next. If you're doing the proper Inner-Forming˝, your subconscious mind is already working on the next step. Relax at such times, and let the situation flow over you.

Don't dismiss out-of-hand the huge, crazy, and whacky thoughts that come to you. Your subconscious is communicating with you, so all ideas should be respected and evaluated. Many of them may not be workable in their initial form, yet they might provide creative alternatives after they are modified.

Journey or Destination?

When you plan for a trip, you have a destination. If you look at a map, you can put your finger on the little dot that is your destination and say, "That's where I want to be." Although the trappings of success are easy to see—more money, healthier body, better clothes, better relationships, bigger house, nicer car—you cannot point out those things and say, "That is success."

Success is not a destination, it's a journey. Once you have reached a particular goal, if you have any heart at all, you have already set another one even higher. The satisfaction that success brings is not in reaching a given point, or even the things that come with having reached that point. Satisfaction comes from becoming the person you want to be, adhering to your values, and enjoying the company of those who have traveled with you.

If you are setting goals and reaching them, then you are successful. The process of moving ever-upward is not one that creates frustration because of an unresolved appetite. The process of success is pleasurable because it's in the nature of human beings to strive to better themselves. That's the positive side for all the bad things I've blamed on being *human* throughout this book!

In the chapter on mentoring, I stated that the mentoring process requires you to be available to mentor someone else. This same principle applies to achieving success. No one succeeds alone, and it's important that you have the proper "attitude of gratitude" about your success. I'm not simply talking about the help from other people, or the efforts that they have put into your success. I'm talking about the universal truth that you owe something to the world. In the past they referred to the concept as *noblesse oblige*, or the obligation of the fortunate to lead and assist those who were less fortunate. More than that, it was the obligation to act nobly in all matters and not simply take good fortune for granted.

Keep in mind the concept of *noblesse oblige*, and in all things— particularly your journey toward success—be worthy.

A Final Word

Even if you don't completely believe in yourself right now, please know that I absolutely believe in you. I believe that

- you have an unlimited amount of potential.

- you have the ability to achieve whatever you want in your life.

- you will be very successful, while helping other people become successful.

- you will continue learning and growing.

- you will make positive differences in other people's lives.

- you will handle your small failures like a true self-leader.

- you are right where you need to be at this very moment.

- you will discover the true beauty within yourself.

- you are now changed forever.

Most of all, I believe that you will truly leap beyond your limits.

(Now continue to the action guide,
set your intention, and get started!)

Appendix A
Action Guide!

Do the following seven steps I've suggested here. Continue doing them without stopping or quitting, and you will be commanding and ruling your own future!

1. Write out your detailed vision of your desired future. Update and rewrite it each and every month.

2. Create a detailed goal statement as described in chapter five. Read your statement every morning and every night. Update and rewrite it each and every month.

3. Choose a few techniques for your Inner-Forming". Then dedicate ten minutes twice each day to sitting quietly with your eyes closed and doing your Inner-Forming".

4. Manage your Outer-Performing" every day. Dedicate five minutes each day to reviewing your daily activities with regards to time management and importance.

5. Study the concept of success a little bit every day by reading books, listening to audio, watching video, attending seminars, etc.

6. Get a coach or a mentor, and meet regularly.

7. Participate in a mastermind group with positive, like-minded individuals. Meet at least once per week.

Appendix B
Exercises and Discussion Points

To get more out of this book, here are some powerful exercises for you to do when your intuition prompts you. I've broken them down by chapter so you can focus your efforts on whichever topic you wish. They can also be used as discussion points within a group.

Chapter One (Prelude to Progress)

- Make a list of things in your life that you'd like to do more of.

- Write out the different roles that you play: father, mother, son, daughter, manager, employee, friend, driver, cook, teacher, etc.

- Find information on where you were five or ten years ago. Look for physical, financial, professional, and emotional markers.

- List skills or talents that you have developed over the last few years.

- List some of your beliefs that you think hold you back (e.g., "I'm too old" or "I'm not good enough").

- List some things that you wanted to do but never did.

Chapter Two (The Birthplace of All Your Actions)

- Think about activities you do that seem to be a waste of energy and time. Think of alternate activities you can do that would move you toward your goals more efficiently.

- Think about some time in the past when you were unable to reach your goal. Consider if you could have done things differently.

- Challenge your beliefs. Consider some of your beliefs that affect your decision making. Now go out and try to find examples that disprove that belief.

- Discover how much noise advertisers put into your head. Go for a day without any media input—no television, radio, newspapers, magazines, or Internet.

- List some of the plans that you had in your mind but that you never fulfilled.

Chapter Three (The Power of the Mind)

- Do research on the powers of the mind. Find instances where people have done seemingly impossible feats using their mind.

- Examine any phobias or irrational fears that you have. Do they stem from earlier experiences? Think about how you can face these fears and overcome them.

- Find a habit that you have that you'd like to change. Treat it as an experiment. Find out what triggers the action, what time of day you partake in it, etc., and see if your focus reduces occurrence of the habit.

- Think about a goal that you would really like to achieve. Picture it as vividly as possible. Now, examine your feelings. Do you feel happy, scared, doubtful? See if you can associate pleasant feeling with the image.

- Identify some of your abilities that you can do very easily but others find difficult. Trace it back to its origin. Why are you able to do it so well? Can you duplicate this method with other actions?

Chapter Four (Taking Command)

- For one day, be active rather than reactive. Refuse to respond reflexively when someone pushes your buttons.

- Examine a situation in which you feel powerless. Find one area that you can exert some control over, and do it.

- Is there an area in which you have not held yourself accountable? Start today to take back that responsibility.

- For one day, keep every promise that you have made—to yourself and to other people.

- Make a list of reasons why you deserve to achieve your big goals.

- Identify an occasion where you spontaneously became a leader when the situation demanded it.

Chapter Five (Your Future, Your Choice)

- Express what your idea of success is in concrete form. Write it down, draw a picture, record your description of it, or cut a photo out of a magazine.

- Take some time to answer this question: If time and money were no object, what would it be possible for me to do?

- Write down all the activities that make you happy. Put them in levels of intensity until you find the one that you're most passionate about, the one you feel you were put on earth to do.

- Make a list of obstacles that you feel prevent you from reaching your potential. Now, examine each obstacle and decide what a really smart, ingenious, and resourceful person would do to overcome it. (Surprise! You're that person!)

- Create a goal statement for the single most important goal in your life. Take the time to be thorough and detailed.

Chapter Six (A Winning Strategy)

- Find a way to cooperate with another person today, even if it's doing something small.

- Examine your actions to see if petty jealousy or envy ever determine what you do. If you find that they do, make changes in your outlook to eliminate them.

- Find a reason to laugh along with someone else.

- Look at the ways you compete with others. Are any of them productive? Eliminate those that are destructive.

- Identify a person whom everyone appreciates. Try to emulate him or her.

- Write down three things you appreciate about each person you work and live with.

Chapter Seven (Inner-Forming˝)

- Observe your self-image in your mind. Mentally change your attributes one at a time (in the image itself) and build yourself up to be the person you wish to be. See yourself performing actions perfectly and enjoying feeling great about it.

- Sit calmly, close your eyes, and visualize your big goals as if you have already achieved them. Make them big and bright. Decide the exact time you will do this every day, and then do it.

- Take a pause and be completely in the moment, like you've slipped out of time. Feel the "now." Observe your surroundings and your own feelings.

- Choose an important action and, before you do it, pause, close your eyes, and set your intention of the outcome you would like your action to create.

Chapter Eight (Outer-Performing˝)

- List 10–20 actions you do every day. Decide which ones are the most critical for achieving your goals. Focus more on those actions, and maybe even eliminate actions that are useless.

- For one week, keep track of all your daily activities and how much time you spend on each one in your job or business. Then add up the time you spent on each different type of activity throughout the week. Evaluate your activity.

- Dedicate some time every day for your continued learning about yourself and your success. Follow your intuition— read books, listen to audio, watch video, speak with your mentor, etc.

- Do something you've never done before to inspire and excite you.

Chapter Nine (Creating Teammates)

- For one day, be as helpful to other people as you possibly can, without thought of reward.

- Write a thank-you note to someone today.

- Engage in conversation with an acquaintance. Find out something about their life that you didn't know. Be genuinely interested in them.

- Examine how your communication changes with the different settings and groups you're in. Note how adaptive your communications are.

- For one day, make an effort to remember the first names of the people you meet.

- In one of your conversations, consciously listen on all levels as best you can.

Chapter Ten (The Art of Not Giving Up)

- Find a task or chore that you've had trouble completing successfully. Determine that today you will finish it, no matter what. Then do it.

- Consciously downplay problems with your language and your mind. For example, if something starts to anger you, don't say you're *furious*, say you're *peeved*.

- Determine if your actions are holding someone else back. Eliminate those actions.

- Find a project that you have put off. Decide that today is the day you're going to start it. Find a small first step that you can do, shake off inertia, and get started.

- Observe and describe your momentum over the last six months. When were you strong and when were you not so strong?

- Make a list of all your small successes from the past week.

Chapter Eleven (The Oracle)

- Select an area in which you want to improve. Look around for someone who has succeeded in that area. Ask that person to lunch (your treat, of course.)

- Make a list of possible mentors for yourself. Make a list of the pluses and minuses of each one, determining if they are the appropriate mentor for you.

- Find an area in which you are strong, and offer to help someone who needs assistance in that area. Use the Socratic method to help them find their own answers.

- Talk with people who are successful. See if they are involved in a mastermind group or if they can recommend one.

- Select a problem you want to resolve. Get with others who are involved with the problem and conduct a brainstorming session.

Chapter Twelve (Falling Then Rising)

- Examine something that you believe you "failed" at. Were your expectations unrealistic? Were the conditions you used to define "success" too precise so that it was impossible to achieve?

- Find a story of someone you admire, and find the obstacles that they had to overcome.

- Examine a setback you've had, and recalibrate your mind so that you can view it as feedback—information to help you adjust your approach so that you can be successful.

- Establish a new habit, one that will move you closer to your goal.

- Identify a mistake you made that bothers you. Then forgive yourself for it and move on.

Chapter Thirteen (Begin to Win)

- Go back through this book with a pencil or pen and a highlighter. Find concepts or passages that appeal to you and highlight them.

- If a comment or passage provokes a question, write the question in the margins.

- Determine if one section or chapter applies to you more than the others and examine why.

- Find quotes or references that appeal to you and look them up on the Internet or in your library.

- Choose one topic in this book and read another book that is devoted solely to that specific topic.

Appendix C
Recommended Books and Movies

Books:

Byways of Blessedness by James Allen

The Science of Getting Rich by Wallace D. Wattles

In Search of Schrödinger's Cat: Quantum Physics and Reality by John Gribbin

The Art of Acting by Stella Adler

As a Man Thinketh by James Allen

The Picture of Dorian Gray by Oscar Wilde

Awaken the Giant Within by Anthony Robbins

The Power of NOW by Eckhart Tolle

You Were Born Rich by Bob Proctor

Tao Te Ching: The Definitive Edition by Lao Tzu (Translation and Commentary by Jonathan Star)

Benjamin Franklin: The Autobiography and Other Writings by Benjamin Franklin

Psycho-Cybernetics: A New Way to Get More Living Out of Life by Maxwell Maltz.

How to Win Friends and Influence People by Dale Carnegie

365 Tao by Deng Ming-Dao

The Memory Book by Harry Lorrayne and Jerry Lucas

Think and Grow Rich by Napoleon Hill

Ishmael by Daniel Quinn

Abraham Lincoln: A Biography by Benjamin P. Thomas

Movies:

Gattaca (1997)

The Illusionist (2006)

What the #$! Do We Know!?* (2004)

Braveheart (1995)

Crouching Tiger, Hidden Dragon (2000)

Rocky (1976)

The Matrix (1999)

The Secret (Extended Edition) (2006)

Beyond the Secret (2009)

Groundhog Day (1993)

Appendix D
A Conversation with Chris Curran

Recently I had the pleasure of being interviewed by my good friend Dan Hollis (author of *The Magic of Selling: A Treasure Map for the Future Successful Salesperson*). Below is an excerpt of the interview. Dan and I have shared the stage many times to help people learn about sales, life, awareness, and self-improvement.

Dan Hollis: This is Dan Hollis, and I have the privilege of sitting here with my good friend Chris Curran. Chris's book is going to be released very soon, within the next couple of months. Hopefully I'll get one of the first copies. I'm elated about it. I have a couple of questions I wanted to ask Chris, and it's going to be incorporated into the back of his book. It's going to give us a little sneak peek into Chris the person. The first thing I would like to ask you, Chris, what is really the purpose of this section of the book? I understand you want to kind of give the reader more of a human feel to you as a person above and beyond all the wonderful information that you're going to be sharing with them. What is the purpose of this section of the book?

Chris Curran: The purpose of this section is, along with the introduction of the book, to put my overall message into perspective. The book itself is the culmination of a lot of work that

I've done, but really my message and my work come from inside me. So knowing more about me could help facilitate a deeper understanding of my overall message.

Hollis: So you're kind of really trying to—again, I think of it as a sneak peek into the real Chris above and beyond Chris the mentor.

Curran: Sure.

Hollis: At another point in time you mentioned to me that the purpose of the book really is to help people, I guess similar to why I wrote my book. What does it mean when you talk about empowerment and working with other human beings?

Curran: My whole life, going back as far as I can remember, I'd never seen anyone or met anyone who was really completely happy. And you know when you're a kid, you're just happy, life is good. So …

Hollis: You don't have responsibilities, really.

Curran: Absolutely. So I observed people, I guess mainly my own family. I did come from a divorced family. That was quite a roller-coaster ride, by the way. But from a very young age, I somehow always knew deep in my heart that people can be truly happy. Life is such a wonderful experience, so why would anyone choose to spend any time being negative or being stuck on a plateau? Humans are creative beings, and as we get older we seem to stop learning and stop growing. We just think, "Well, this is what I am, and this is all I am," but I don't buy that. I never bought that. I challenge that.

Hollis: It's easy for people to wallow in self-pity when they're not in a good place in their mind. You try to get them out of that place.